The Whole Man
Meditations on the Life of Christ

William Reams
Our Lady of the Holy Spirit Abbey
2625 Highway 212 S.W.
Conyers, GA 30094-4044

The Whole Man: Meditations on the Life of Christ
By Brother William Reams, O.C.R.
Our Lady of the Holy Spirit Monastery
With the permission of the Superior

Third Printing

Printed in the United States of America.

Published by
Ann R. Griffin Graphic Design
718 S. Bella Vista Street
Tampa, Florida 33609

International Standard Book Number 0-9669329-0-0

Cover painting by John Gutcher, Tampa, Florida

The Whole Man
Meditations on the Life of Christ

Jesus Christ,
a Man like
us in all
things but sin
Hebrews 4, 15

The Scripture quotations are mostly taken from the Confraternity of Christian Doctrine Translation, 1941, and the Good News for Modern Man translation, 1966, and are frequently paraphrased, often without quotation marks.

To All the Martyrs of Algeria,
especially Pierre Clavérie,
Bishop of Oran

and the Cistercian Monks,
Christian de Chergé
Luc Dochier
Christophe Lebreton
Michel Fleury
Bruno Lemarchand
Célestin Ringeard
Paul Favre Miville

Preface

The Imitation of Christ says that the whole life of Jesus in this world was a Cross and a martyrdom. The cowardly disciples, the fickle crowds, the Pharisees and Sadducees, the Scribes and Lawyers, the High Priests Annas and Caiaphas, Herod, Pilate, Judas - and the devil, all teamed up to make it that.

This book tells the story of Jesus' struggle. Yet it is not a scholarly "Life of Christ," which the Scripture scholars say cannot be written in any case. It is not even "A Meditative Life of Christ." It is simply a combination of what I call "the story of Jesus" and some meditations on certain principal aspects of that story.

In a sense it does unfold the life of Christ. Yet it still may be considered simply an attempt to make the Gospel a bit more readable by means of meditations on the developing story - and as such it has the disadvantage of leaving out much that is important.

But beneath the chronological development of the Gospel story, there is also a very distinct drama in progress, and this is what I have tried to bring out. On the deepest level, Jesus was struggling not so much against the Jewish religious leaders of His day as against "principalities and powers, the evil spirits in the heavens, the world rulers of this darkness." We must always remember this in reading the Gospels. Indeed, it might truly be said that we ourselves are just as responsible for Jesus' death as were the Jews of His time. And Scripture itself remarks that the Gentiles also played just as much a role in crucifying Jesus as the Jews did.

However, there is still a third thing I have tried to do - and this, I think, is the most important of all. I have tried to emphasize how Jesus' victory as Man over the powers of evil - He came into this world "to destroy the works of the devil" - was based on His absolute holiness and moral integrity, which themselves resulted in a human wholeness that was truly wonderful.

In the end we are enabled to transcend, in a certain sense, all the terrible labor of the struggle, and simply rest quietly in the prayerful contemplation of this wonderful wholeness of Jesus Christ. He can truly be said to be the Principle of all human moral, intellectual and spiritual integrity as the Whole Man *par excellence*, really the only Whole Man, who shares His wholeness with us all.

The Whole Man
Meditations on the Life of Christ

PART ONE
THE HOLY CHILD

PART TWO
THE WHOLE MAN

PART THREE
INTEGRITY

Introduction

Faith in Jesus Christ

In the Apostles' Creed, after professing faith "in God, the Father Almighty," we go on to affirm that we believe "in Jesus Christ, His only Son, our Lord, who was conceived by the the Holy Spirit, born of the Virgin Mary, suffered under Pontius Pilate, was crucified, died, and was buried. He descended into hell. The third day He rose again from the dead. He ascended into Heaven and sits at the right hand of God, the Father Almighty. From thence He shall come to judge the living and the dead."

The Catholic Church teaches that without this faith in Jesus Christ there is no salvation, though, of course, all who seek God with a sincere heart, but through no fault of theirs do not know the Gospel teaching also are saved by Jesus through their "implicit" faith in Him. And St. Thomas Aquinas says that our first approach to God is precisely through faith. Let us meditate for a few moments, then, on the Mystery of our Christian Faith, our faith in "this Jesus, whom I crucified....who loved me and gave Himself up for me."

Jesus Christ was born of the Virgin Mary, by the power of the Holy Spirit, in the little town of Bethlehem in Judea in the land of Palestine 2,000 years ago. He was born a little Baby just as all of us are born. He was born in poverty, in a stable cave out under the stars, in the middle of a dark and beautiful, but chilly night.

His miraculous birth was announced by an angel to some shepherds, poor like Him, spending the night with their flocks in the fields nearby. They came and adored Him, and understood.

Later, Magi came from the East, and they too adored Him and presented Him with royal gifts of gold, frankincense and myrrh - gold for the Great King that He was, frankincense in honor of His Divinity, and myrrh for His burial as the Crucified Redeemer of Man.

Many would believe in Jesus. Mary was the first to believe. Joseph, her husband, likewise believed. The shepherds and the Magi believed.

Many would refuse to believe. Herod the King did not believe, and tried to murder the Child. In the sickness of his mind, he saw in this little Baby, whose Kingdom was not of this world, a threat to his own ruthlessly acquired security.

Elizabeth, Mary's older cousin, had believed, and Zachary, her husband. Their son, the great John the Baptizer, had leapt for joy even in his mother's womb at the presence of Mary and the Divine Infant in her own womb.

Peter and Andrew and James and John the Apostle would believe. The Pharisees and Sadducees and Scribes and Lawyers would not believe. Mary Magdalen would believe with all the most ardent love of her whole heart. Annas and Caiaphas and a later Herod and Pontius Pilate and Judas would not believe. Stephen and Paul and Barnabas and Mark and Luke would believe.

Some would believe, and some would not believe. Many would believe, and many more would not believe.

For faith in Jesus Christ is a most mysterious grace, a sheer gift of the all good, all wise, all powerful God.

What is it? The grace of living faith is a sharing in the Divine Nature, as St. Peter says. It is a participation in God's own Life of knowledge and love. It is "the substance of the things we must hope for, a conviction about things we cannot see." This grace of living faith in Jesus Christ our Lord is the substance of the Beatifying Vision of "the Divine Essence" that we will have in Heaven by "the Light of Glory." Grace and Glory are substantially the same thing. By the grace of living faith we know and love Jesus Christ and the Father He has revealed in Their Common Holy Spirit even in this world, though in much darkness and obscurity. By the Light of Glory we will see this Triune God face to face in Heaven in unutterable and unending Happiness.

Faith is likewise a conviction - that the Man Christ Jesus whom we contemplate in the pages of the Gospel, moving throughout Galilee and Judea, doing good to all - *Pertransiit benefaciendo* - is truly God, the Divine Son of the Divine Father, and our Savior.

By the grace of living faith we believe in the Divinity of Jesus Christ and in His power and loving will to save us from hell and lead us to the holiness of perfect love for Him. We trust in His word, "who can neither deceive nor be deceived." We believe in His wondrous promises, "Ask and you shall receive, seek and you shall find...." We believe in His Person, in Him Himself, Jesus Christ, our Lord and God, and our faith is our confidence.

Living faith is a virtue, but also a profound Mystery. It is an obedience, "obedience to the truth....obedience to Jesus Christ." St. Peter says that we are "children of obedience." St. Paul says that it is "the obedience of faith" that makes us the true children of Abraham, "our father in faith." The age of circumcision came and went. The faith of Abraham, "who believed, and it was credited to him as justice," lives on in us his spiritual children, "spiritual Semites."

"Abraham rejoiced to see my day. He saw it and was glad." Such is the power of faith. Faith sees in the darkness. In the darkness of the night faith sees Someone.

In the darkness of this world, faith in Him sees Jesus Christ, our Lord and our God. And by this faith in Jesus, as St. Augustine said, "we touch God," and are made whole by that touch.

And then we are enabled to say with the great Paul himself, "I live now, no longer I, the sick man, but Christ lives in me, the Whole Man."

Part One

The Holy Child

I

She Brought Forth Her Firstborn Child

The Mystery of Jesus begins with Mary, His Virgin Mother, just as it concludes with her present in the upper room at Pentecost. Mary brings Him into our world by her "Yes," her "*Fiat.*" She said to the Angel Gabriel, "I am the maidservant of the Lord. Let it be done to me as you say." And the Word was made flesh in her womb, and took even fuller possession of her Immaculate Heart and Soul.

It is always Mary who brings Jesus into the world, as the all pure Bride of His Holy Spirit. He is her "Firstborn Child." All of us are "children in the Child," Jesus.

She brought forth her little Son, "and laid Him in a manger, because there was no room for them in the inn."

Jesus Christ came into our world through Mary. He came "to destroy the works of the devil" - and already on the night of His birth He was beginning His work. His angels were announcing "good news of great joy for all people" to a band of simple shepherds who were "keeping watch over their flocks by night" in fields not far away. The glory of God lit up the night sky for a few moments, and He wished His people peace.

The angels left, and the shepherds went over to

Bethlehem "to see this thing" that the Lord had made known to them. They found "the Sign," the Baby, wrapped round and laid in a manger, together with Mary and Joseph. They adored and understood the Mystery of God.

+

The gift of understanding is given only to the simple and humble, to the heart that does not deny what it sees. The Magi came, and they too adored and understood. They worshipped, and left their gifts of treasures, and went away filled with the gifts of wisdom and understanding, knowledge and piety, fortitude and fear, and the counsel of the Holy Spirit not to return to Herod, but to go back to their home "by another way."

The shepherds and the Magi teach us how to approach Jesus Christ. They preach to us very quietly always to seek Him out together with Mary and Joseph. They teach us to find Him where He really is, in poverty and peace. They point out to us, silently, the wholeness of the straw on which He lies, and the cool night air, and the shining stars.

They tell us, without saying a word, that we do not need the wealth of this world. We only need the Sacrament of Jesus, and Mary to keep us faithful to Him, and Joseph to keep us true to both of them.

We only need the wonderful Holy Spirit of Christmas, to keep us children all the days of our life. We only need to be little children and kneel before the Christmas crib and love the Divine Child, as he rests in the arms of Mary, His Mother and ours, and Joseph watches faithfully through the night.

+

The shepherds leave, and the Magi leave, and the Child must be circumcised. For coming into the world He had said to His Father, "In the head of the Book it is written of me, that I should do Your will, O my God." He had prayed, "Sacrifice and oblation You did not desire. Then I said, 'Behold, I come to do Your will, my God.'"

"A Body You have fitted to me," a Body that could suffer, a Body that could shed its Precious Blood for the sins of men - a Body that would shed all its Blood.

For the present it would only be a little bit. Yet the pain would be great. It would be pain shed in solidarity with poor helpless sinners.

And then it would heal, and the Baby Boy, "the Firstborn male opening the womb," would be taken by His parents to be presented in the Temple. And the All Pure Virgin would go there to be purified also. Together with Joseph, Jesus and Mary would offer the sacrifice of the poor, "a pair of turtle doves, or two young pigeons."

And "the holy old man, Simeon" would bless God and take the Child in his arms and call Him the Sign of Contradiction. He would announce to Mary that a sword would pierce her own soul, that the deepest intentions of many hearts might rise to the surface.

+

After King Herod's massacre of the Holy Innocents, and his subsequent death, Mary and Joseph would return from their flight into Egypt and would settle with their

Baby in Nazareth. The Child would grow and become strong and wise, in favor with both God and men.

When He reached the age of twelve, they would take Him with them on their annual Passover pilgrimage to the Temple in Jerusalem, to His Father's House once again. And He would linger behind, irresistibly attracted there. And after three days they would find Him "sitting in the midst of the Doctors, listening to them and asking them questions." These "Doctors of the Law" were "amazed at His intelligence and His answers." And then He would very simply and humbly and submissively return to Nazareth and remain obedient to Mary and Joseph, until His time had come.

Such is the Mystery of the Holy Childhood as the Gospels present it to us. It is an infinite Mystery, a Divine Mystery, a Mystery of Beauty and Love, of Silence and Prayer. Year in and year out, the Holy Family live together a quiet and obscure life of poverty, simplicity and labor. It is a life well known by the multitudes of poor families throughout the world. It is the life that produces the real leaders of the world. It is the life of virtue.

It is a very difficult life. The life of a poor family can be terribly difficult. Who can guess the martyrdom of Joseph? It has been said that "habits are wonderful things - they make life easy for us." But contrary to settled habit, Joseph was always being called upon by God in a dream to pick up in the middle of the night and head off somewhere far distant. Joseph's life was completely unpredictable, because he was led so completely by the Spirit of God. And after he finally settled with Mary and the Child in Nazareth, there was the martyrdom of providing honestly for his little family in a dishonest world. Truly is he the patron saint of fathers and the protector of virgins.

The life of the Holy Family, as the common life of all the world's poor, was a hard life. Yet even so, it was a blessedly happy and holy life, because it was a life of prayer and perfect submission to the will of God.

+

The shepherds had been afraid at the tremendous vision of God's mighty angels. Perhaps the Magi too knew fear in their caution not to be discovered by Herod as they outwitted his desire to murder the Child. Mary and Joseph were filled with fear, not only for themselves, but for their Baby, as they fled into Egypt.

The coming of God into our world was not unaccompanied by the very common human reality of fear.

Yet it brought peace to a fearful world. The "*Pax Romana*," though not at all a bad thing, was yet a purely material peace. The Incarnation of the Son of God would bring an infinitely deeper peace, peace deep down within human hearts.

Peace would be the proper and peculiar gift of Jesus Christ.

The Prince of Peace would bring peace to Mary and Joseph, the shepherds and the Magi, and all who desired it. But He would also bring joy.

"I bring you good news of great joy," the angel had said. Father Pierre Teilhard de Chardin has said that "Joy is the most infallible sign of the presence of God." It was fitting that when God came into this world to be born of Mary in order to take away all our sins, there should be great joy. A Savior had been born, and He would be given the name "Jesus," because that's what it means.

The shepherds had gone their way "glorifying and praising God for all that they had heard and seen." Theirs was a lasting joy, the joy of the poor, who could recognize real Wealth when they found it.

This Joy of the shepherds, and of the Magi, was really Jesus, who remained with Mary and Joseph as the Peace that is joy's perfection, a quietly joyful Peace in which they slept and rose again, throughout the years.

+

God loves us - that is the Gospel, "the Good News." Jesus Christ is the Incarnation of God's Love for us. It is so hard to believe in His love for us. The world, the flesh and the devil all say, "He doesn't love you. He's mean. He's strict. If you go back to Him after you've sinned, He'll be angry and bawl you out."

But Mary and Joseph say to us, "No! Behold the Infant God! Behold what He has become for love of you. Behold the Goodness of the Lord. Behold His Mercy and His Love, and do not be afraid of Him. Rather, come and kneel with us, and let us worship and adore together and give Him our hearts. In return He will give us His profound and lasting, joyful and blessed peace."

And so we kneel quietly beside the Christmas crib, and we discover in the depths of our hearts that it is really true, that God is Love, and all He can do is love and give gifts, the gift of all things in the Gift of Himself.

With the angels and the shepherds and the Magi, we give "glory to God," and He gives peace to us. It is a "wondrous exchange." We give Him a human nature, together with all our weaknesses and sins, and He gives us a share in His own Divine Goodness, Life and Joy. We give "glory to God" by humbly acknowledging that we really have nothing to give Him except what He has given us. We really have nothing to give Him but the surrender of our hearts.

And with this small gift of His child, the Lord of Glory is pleased. We "children in the Child" offer ourselves along with Jesus' offering. His life stretches out ahead of Him, nor is our own in this world yet completed. In union with Him, we offer ourselves to the will of the Father for the salvation of all.

Jesus will suffer and die for the sins of the world. We too offer ourselves to be transformed into instruments of peace. We too by our sufferings, united to His, will be able to bring the graces of salvation and holiness to our own little sector of the vast fields that are "white for the harvest."

In our own hidden life, so much like that of Jesus, Mary and Joseph at Nazareth, we will work and struggle and suffer "for the salvation of the whole world."

+

Jesus Christ is "the Firstborn" of many brothers and sisters. And Mary is the Mother of us all. She gave Him birth, and she gives us birth, in Him. She is the Mother of what St. Augustine called "the whole man....the whole Christ," the whole Church.

There was a lot that she did not understand about the

Mystery of Christmas. She reflected much on all that she saw and heard and experienced. She lived by faith. She had joy, but it was joy in the Holy Spirit, not in complete understanding. We too have "joy in Jesus," even without completely understanding. We know that He loves us, that He has come to save us and make us holy, and that He is powerful enough to do it all, and that is enough for us.

We believe in Jesus Christ, whom, as St. Peter says, we have never seen. Yet we have seen the Mystery of Christmas, and our hearts tell us that it is so utterly beautiful that it absolutely must be true. For the night that God came into the world, the darkness was brilliantly illumined by His glory and brightened by the sweet song of myriads of angels. It was a wondrous brightness that did not pass entirely away even when the angels returned to Heaven, a brightness that lived on in the warm glow of Joseph's lantern and the Face of the Infant God.

The Light had come into the world, and the darkness had not comprehended it. The darkness had not understood and had not responded, but it was incapable of extinguishing the Light. The Light lives on in the Eucharistic Jesus, in His Holy Spirit in the Community of the Church, in the hearts of all the baptized faithful.

The Light that was born into our world on that first Christmas Eve lives on in the hearts of all who believe. It is the Light of Life, the Living Light.

It lives on in all who, like the Holy Family at Nazareth, go on from day to day in the darkness of fidelity to duty, in the way of work and prayer, in obedience to God.

+

The shepherds and the Magi were the worthy envoys of the whole world of Jews and Gentiles. Willingly if unwittingly, they brought our hearts to the worship of the Newborn King.

Simeon and Anna were the representatives of all who would accept this King with love and joy. The Doctors in the Temple would be merely the first to wonder and marvel at the Truth He brought to us in His own Person.

"No one ever spoke the way this Man speaks." And no one ever will again. He was Jesus, the Revealer of the Father. To see Him was to see "the good God." To hear Him was to hear the Eternal Wisdom. To be healed by Him was to be saved.

He heals us quietly as we kneel beside His crib. We touch Him by faith, and power comes out from this little Baby and makes us whole.

Jesus Christ, the Son of the Father, comes down from Heaven into our messy, sinful world, and the Gospel tells us that now "God is with us." His presence among us has put this hopeless globe into the Path of salvation. We had all but given up, and then God Himself arrived with the grace and gift of holy hope.

With the shepherds and the Magi, with Simeon and Anna, with the learned Doctors of the Law, we contemplate this Holy and Mysterious Child, and we are rejuvenated. New life surges through the very veins of our bodies. We cannot help thrilling at the realization of what has happened, and what now will never stop happening.

God has become One of us. Heaven and earth, the Divine and the human, are wedded in the Person of Jesus Christ. We are no longer alone. "Emmanuel" means "God-with-us."

"This Jesus," obedient day by day to Mary and Joseph, living together with them year in and year out in the little out of the way village of Nazareth in Galilee, is God among us.

+

Since the Incarnation of the Son of God, Jesus Christ our Lord, God is with us truly and completely and eternally. He remains with us in the Most Blessed Sacrament and Sacrifice of the Eucharist and in His wonderful Holy Spirit both among us all in the community and within our individual hearts and souls by the stupendous gift of grace.

By the gifts of Uncreated and Sanctifying Grace, God Himself lives within us and grants us a created sharing in His own Divine Life.

God is with us, fully and completely, ever since Mary our Mother said "Yes" to His proposal of love through the Angel Gabriel. Mary said "*Fiat*," "Let it be," and it happened. God came to live among us. He "pitched His tent in our midst."

Non horruisti Virginis uterum. O Lord Jesus, You did not shudder at the thought of entering the Virgin's womb and being enclosed there for nine full months. Nor do You shudder at the thought of being lovingly imprisoned in the tabernacles of our churches. For You are the Lord our God, infinite in every respect, and You mercifully encompass all who embrace You, Your truth and Your will.

You do not shudder at the thought of entering our bodies in Holy Communion, but it is really You who transform us into Yourself, so that ever more and more "we live and move and have our being" within You, our Omnipresent King.

God is with us, ever since Mary conceived Him in her womb. He appeared among us when she gave Him birth. He lived among us as a Child, a Youth, a young Man. He died and rose again, then disappeared at the Ascension only to return to us again with infinitely greater fullness in His Most Holy Spirit at Pentecost. And now He is perfectly with us "all days, even to the consummation of the world."

+

St. Thomas Aquinas said that the wonder of the Incarnation, together with the glory of Heaven and the greatness of Mary, is one of the three works of His that God just simply could not improve on. In the Incarnate Word, He gave us All He had, All He is. It is the Mystery of God that each Divine Person is as great as all Three together, because They live completely in One Another. In the little Baby that Mary holds close to her nursing breasts dwells "All the Fullness of the Godhead corporeally." Whoever sees this young Boy working quietly with Joseph and mastering the carpenter's trade sees the Father. For it pleased the Father to have All His Fullness dwell in the Incarnate Jesus.

God could not, cannot, give us any more than He already has given us in "this Jesus." As St. John of the Cross emphasizes, He has nothing more to say to us. He has said All in His one Word, Jesus. It is not that He does not want to say more to us, because He knows it would not do any good. It is simply that there is nothing more for Him to say.

In Jesus Christ born of the Virgin Mary and crucified for our salvation, God the Father says to us, "See how I love you! See how infinitely much I love you! To redeem you from your sins I delivered up my only Son. From now on, if you will only go to Him and let yourself be transformed into Him, I look at you and see no longer a sinful 'child of wrath,' but 'only Jesus,' my Beloved Child."

He says to us, "I have loved you with an everlasting love. Therefore I have drawn you to Him, that He may speak to you my infinite love for you in a human way that you can understand."

He says to us, "Look at Jesus, the helpless little Infant, the Victim of love nailed to the Cross, and see my infinite love for you. See His love for Me and for you. And turn from evil into the path of goodness, that you may not destroy your immortal soul, but may be happy with Him and with Me in the Blessed Unity of Our Holy Spirit for ever and ever."

+

We must gaze long and intently at the Divine Baby who sleeps silently in the stable crib or nurses quietly at Mary's breasts, or is carried lovingly in her arms or Joseph's.

We must long consider this growing Boy, as he becomes strong and wise in the ways of men. We must look long and intently on this Jesus, "the Author and Finisher of our faith," as He goes very simply about the chores of His hidden life. He is obedient to Mary and Joseph. He is "subject" to them. He subjects His mind and His will. And this Divine Child says to us, "Learn of me, for I am meek and humble of heart."

We are children of God, and if we never come to realize it and live consciously as His children, we will never enter the Kingdom of Heaven. But He Himself has become a Child, in order to teach us that it's "okay." It's okay to be a child. It's all right.

"Be children in evil, and in mind mature." There was nothing silly about the Child Jesus. There was only a calm and quiet innocence. There was perfect simplicity and a wisdom ever becoming more and more complete.

Indeed, this Child was from the beginning more truly mature than any of us ever will be.

And yet He was a simple little Child.

He grew and became a thoughtful Boy. He was intelligent. Yet Rome knew nothing of His intelligence, or even Antioch. The Doctors of the Law were amazed by it, but that day passed, and though perhaps they never forgot the amazing Lad who had astounded them that day, yet the world at large did not hear much or anything about the incident. It was Mary, turning it over and over in her Heart, who passed it on to St. Luke, and to us.

This Boy was a Mystery, yet a very quiet One.

+

He had said on coming into the world that He was coming to do His Father's will. And He was doing it. He was doing the will of Mary and Joseph. He who created the wood was learning to shape it. He who gave existence and thought and the gift of grace to Mary and Joseph willed to learn from them the art of surviving as One of God's poor.

It seems that Mary and Joseph 'home-schooled' Jesus in the Scriptures. It was under them that He made His first contact with the inspired Books of His people. And what He had known from Eternity He began to learn in time. What He had eternally understood, He began to penetrate deeply with His human mind. The Love that He had savored throughout endless ages of Divine Triune "Circumincession" He began to experience now "also" in an ever more and more fully human way.

As a little Boy, He began the study of the Word that He was.

By the time He was twelve years old, He had penetrated its Mystery so deeply that the most learned Rabbis of Jerusalem marveled at His profound insight, at such wisdom as they had never encountered before.

This Boy's mind and Heart were bottomless abysses of Mystery. And Mary and Joseph lived with Him daily, and learned from Him. His Father had given them to Him to obey. And in doing so, He learned as a Human Being, grew in the experience of human things. The awesome Lord of Sinai learned from Joseph how to be a carpenter, but without being taught by Joseph, for as St. Thomas Aquinas says, no creature can teach God anything.

Jesus is the only real Teacher, even when He teaches Himself. Even the Infant, nursing at Mary's breasts, had silently taught her secrets of love that can only be called Divine.

+

The Child Jesus, the Boy Jesus, grew humanly. He studied the Sacred Scriptures, and He who had given them to His people and to the world read there the Mysterious Plan of His Father, the Plan that centered completely around Him. He saw it unfolding through the ages, even to Himself studying in the little synagogue.

But already He was acquiring habits of solitude and prayer. He would go off by Himself and "consider the lilies of the field" and commune quietly with His Father.

He had come to save the world, to bless it, not to destroy it. "God so loved the world as to send His only Son." And the Son too loved the world. He loved His people. He loved people in general, in the truth.

He loved the Truth. He who was the Truth adhered to it always with His whole Being. He was not gushy and sentimental. Neither was He overly solemn. He was serious but gentle. He was kind without being soft. He was firm yet open. He was candid yet sincere. He was whole.

He was Divine, and He was Human. He was perfectly Human, more truly and deeply human than we are. He was reflective and moderate, temperate and restrained, yet normal and "natural." He was utterly good, without yielding principle. He was Truth so true that it was a Miracle. He was the Truth that had come into our world to drive out forever the darkness of error and falsehood.

He grew and became a young Man. He worked in Joseph's shop quietly and well, prayerfully. He made good things. But always His life of prayer and communion with His Father was the soul of His whole existence.

He was waiting. He was working as He waited, and praying. He was awaiting the call of His Father. He was awaiting "His hour."

He was patient and self-controlled, perfectly self-possessed. He was the Mystery of the God-Man, living, working, praying - quietly with Mary and Joseph.

+

But the time was drawing near. He was nearly thirty now. Joseph had died "in the arms of Jesus and Mary." Jesus lived with His Mother. He was no longer a little Boy. Yet He had not left her side. They were very close. Yet it was a very disciplined closeness. She knew Him well, even though there were infinitely profound depths that even she could not really enter into.

Still, it is true to say that they knew each other. Their life together was quiet and regular - work and prayer and simplicity.

Patience was for them the passing of the days. Jesus was waiting. Mary comprehended only a deeper and more solemn quietness. Yet she sensed that He was waiting.

He awaited the call of His Father, and she waited for Him and with Him.

The days were quiet, almost still. The work had to be done and was done. But prayer, which had always been everything, was becoming even more the whole of their lives.

Their lives were one life. His life was hers. Her Heart beat with His. There was really only one Heart. It was the obedient Heart of two who had now become more one than ever.

They spoke little. Silence was prayer.

And then - the word reached Nazareth. Jesus' cousin, John, was preaching repentance and baptizing with a baptism of repentance at the Jordan River down south to the east of Judea.

And Jesus knew that now it was time. And Mary sensed the beginning of something new, something she could not understand, and He did not and could not explain to her.

But He had to leave. He was no longer a Child. He was a Man, with a Man's work to do. He was leaving this Woman who had brought Him into the world, had nursed Him as a Baby, had watched over His first steps, had reared Him to youth and young adulthood.

He left her. She watched Him as He walked away. Her eyes followed Him until He passed out of her view.

Jesus, the Son of Mary, the Son of Man, was moving south down the road to Judea and Bethany where John was preaching and baptizing.

And "a Woman wrapped in silence" prayed her lonely prayer in the solitude of a Heart so empty that it seemed to be filled only with death.

Part Two

The Whole Man

II

The Voice of One Crying in the Desert

It was the fifteenth year of the reign of Tiberius Caesar. Pontius Pilate was Procurator in Judea. A new Herod was Tetrarch of Galilee, his brother Philip Tetrarch of the region of Iturea and Trachonitis, and Lysanias Tetrarch of Abiline. The Jewish high priests were Annas and Caiaphas. So does St. Luke place the time when the Word of God had come to John the son of Zachary in the desert.

John had come into the whole region of the Jordan preaching a baptism of repentance for the forgiveness of sins "as it is written in the book of Isaiah the prophet:

> 'The voice of one crying in the desert:
> Prepare the way of the Lord,
> make straight His paths.
> Every valley will be filled in,
> and every mountain and hill will be brought low,
> and the crooked ways shall be made straight,
> and the rough ways smooth,
> and all mankind shall see the salvation of God.' "

John too was a mystery of virtue. He wore "a garment

of camel's hair, with a leather belt around his waist," and he lived on locusts and wild honey.

All Judea and Jerusalem were going out to him to be baptized in the Jordan, "confessing their sins." Many of the Pharisees and Sadducees came to him, and he told them firmly to prove that they were really repentant by producing fruits worthy of a genuine change of heart. He warned them that "every tree that does not bring forth good fruit will be cut down and thrown into the fire."

The crowds asked John, "What should we do?" He told them, "Whoever has two tunics should share with the man who has none. Whoever has food should do the same."

The tax collectors came and asked him, "What should we do?" He told them to exact no more than had been appointed them.

The soldiers said, "And we - what are we to do?" He told them, "Don't treat people roughly, nor accuse anyone falsely. Be content with your pay."

The people were all excited and wondering if John might be the Messiah. So Priests and Levites came to him from Jerusalem and asked him, "Who are you?"

John answered, "I'm not the Messiah." They asked him, "What, then? Are you Elijah?" He said, "I am not." They asked, "Are you the Prophet?" This was "the Prophet like Moses" who was to come. John answered, "No."

They asked him, "Who are you? So we can give an answer to those who sent us. What have you got to say of yourself?" John told them, "I am the voice of one crying in the desert, 'Make straight the way of the Lord,' as Isaiah the prophet said."

These envoys of the Pharisees asked him, "Then why

do you baptize if you're not the Messiah, nor Elijah, nor the Prophet?" John answered, "I am baptizing with water, but in your midst there has stood One whom you do not know." He went on, "One mightier than I is coming, the strap of whose sandals I am not worthy to loose. He will baptize you with the Holy Spirit and with fire."

St. Luke says that it was the very Gospel that John was preaching.

+

"Then," says St. Matthew, "Jesus came from Galilee to John, at the Jordan, to be baptized by him." John was bewildered. He said to Jesus, "It's I that ought to be baptized by You, and you come to me?" Jesus said to him, "Let it be so for now, for thus it becomes us to fulfill all justice." Then John acquiesced.

And the Gospel says, "When Jesus had been baptized, He immediately came up from the water. And behold, the heavens were opened, and He saw the Spirit of God descending as a Dove" upon Himself. Then a voice from the heavens said, "This is my Beloved Son, in whom I am well pleased."

Thus was Jesus' mission inaugurated. He had descended into the waters of the Jordan to be baptized in solidarity with poor sinners. He had cleansed those waters and made them lifegiving. And as He rose up out of them, He was raising up the world along with Himself. His sacrament of water and the Holy Spirit would mean "new creation" for all who would accept it.

But Jesus did not delay at the Jordan. Shortly afterwards, the Scriptures say, He was "driven" by the Holy Spirit into the desert, for His first encounter with the devil. He would be "tempted" three times by this enemy of mankind.

Then the devil would leave Him, and angels would come and minister to His hunger, after His fasting of "forty days and forty nights."

+

After His fast Jesus returned to John at the Jordan. John saw Him coming and said, "Look! The Lamb of God, who takes away the sin of the world! This is He of whom I said, 'After me there comes One who has been set above me, because He was before me.' And I did not know Him. But that He may be known to Israel is why I have come baptizing with water."

John went on, "I saw the Spirit descending as a Dove from Heaven and resting on Him. I didn't know Him, but He who had sent me to baptize with water said to me, 'He on whom you shall see the Spirit descending and resting, He it is who baptizes with the Holy Spirit.' I have seen and borne witness that this is the Son of God."

The following day John was standing there in the same place with two of his disciples. And looking on Jesus as He walked by again, he repeated, "There is the Lamb of God!" And the two disciples heard him speak, and followed Jesus.

We know the story of the Apostles Andrew and John, and how they stayed with Jesus the rest of that day.

Jesus would gather many more disciples and later speak to them of the greatness of John the Baptizer. After

Herod had shut John up in prison for accusing him of adultery with his brother's wife, Herod would finally murder John to please the sinful Herodias. But that is an obscene story that we don't need to tell again here.

Here we need only recall Jesus' praise of John, the greatest of the prophets, "and more than a prophet." Jesus would ask the crowds, "What did you go out into the desert to see?" Not an elegant playboy, not a spineless reed that the breeze could bend any way it blew - but a man, a real man, a profoundly great man, him of whom the Scripture had said, "I am sending my messenger before You, to prepare Your way."

Jesus would tell the Pharisees that John had been a lamp, "burning and shining." They had found satisfaction in enjoying him for awhile.

But by then John had done his work. He had introduced the Bride to the Bridegroom, and after that there was nothing left for him to do but decrease. This was his joy, and it was complete.

Yet John, as great as he was, lived by faith, just as all the rest of us do. And before he died he had sent messengers to Jesus, asking if He really was "the One who was to come - or should we look for some other?" Jesus told them to "Go and report to John what you have seen - the blind receiving back their sight, the deaf their hearing, the lame walking, lepers being cleansed, the poor hearing good news." He said lovingly for them to tell John, "Blessed is the man who does not lose confidence in me."

John did not lose confidence. He died in this faith and confidence, beheaded in the darkness of a dank dungeon cell - the great Precursor of God.

+

Jesus loved John, more than any other human being except Mary and Joseph. John's was a lonely task. He lived his faith in the desert and died alone. There was no glory for him at all in this world. Yet he himself tells us that at the end of his life's work there was joy, joy in all its fullness, the joy of the hero. He gave Israel the Bride to her God. He was the friend of the Bridegroom.

His birth had been announced by an angel, even before that of Jesus. Zachary his father, with inspired words, had declared that he would be great. He would go before the Lord in the spirit and power of Elijah to prepare for Him a people well disposed. He would lead God's people into the way of peace.

Six months along in the womb of his Mother Elizabeth, he would receive the grace and gift of joy from Jesus, likewise hidden in the womb of Mary. At Mary's word of greeting to Elizabeth, the wonderful Holy Spirit would cause the Infant John to leap with happiness within the womb itself.

John never lost that happiness. He grew, and "was in the deserts until the day of his manifestation to Israel." It was an extremely austere happiness. It was the happiness of the greatest of all human beings after Mary and Joseph. It was what St. Paul would later call "all joy and peace in believing."

For John, love consisted in believing in Jesus, in the darkness, in the dungeon, unto death. How terrible was the martyrdom of John! How blind his faith! How great a man!

Jesus loved him. And John loved Jesus. But his love was all faith, in the darkness. John's work was to despoil himself of all his followers, to send everyone to Jesus, and then to die alone, in the awful solitude of pure, unseeing faith. He did it, and he did it perfectly.

+

John decreased, until there was nothing left of him but a headless trunk, sprawled over the filthy floor of a lightless, airless cell deep down in the depths of Herod's desert fortress. This was John's victory, to be slaughtered as the Lamb he had pointed out would be slaughtered. The sinless John, dying in faith and in total physical isolation, stood to the end behind the words he had spoken to his disciples Andrew and another John.

He had realized and understood that no one can do more than Heaven gives him the gift of doing. He had never failed to proclaim that he was not the Messiah, only the forerunner. When disciples of his had complained that Jesus, through His disciples, was becoming a rival Baptizer, he simply replied that this was what was to be expected.

The nobility of John is a bottomless well, a tower of infinite loftiness. Yet he existed only as a relationship to Jesus. He knew that he was nothing, and that the God-Man was all. When we read the Gospels, we sense how perfectly pleased Jesus was with John. For John and Mary Magdalen Jesus had deep and obvious affection.

We could meditate a long, long time on the greatness of John. The more we consider his vocation and his work, the more we are astounded at the challenge he succeeded in meeting fully and completely.

He lived alone and died alone. He made disciples only

to hand them on to Another. He taught Israel to pass on from him to the One his words pointed out. He lived only for Christ and chose deliberately the way of self-annihilation.

He was strong enough to be gentle, but too true to compromise. He spoke out alone against a whole society - and people heard him, and feared God, and responded in faith by being baptized, "confessing their sins."

John's courage was complete. Hardly had he appeared on the banks of the Jordan when he began announcing that his mission was to disappear before the One who was coming after him.

John preached the coming of Christ. In this lay his greatness. He believed in the New Covenant without comprehending it. He stood at the end of an era and on the threshold of a new age, proclaiming it in the sheerest faith. He had left behind all that was familiar. The desert was his only friend, the desert and the God of the desert.

He had cut himself off from the whole of society in order to be able to see the Truth, when the Truth walked into view. He saw Him who is the Truth, saw Him with pure eyes, the penetrating eyes of a perfectly pure heart, and declared to all who would hear, "Look! There is the Lamb of God!"

+

How much did John understand? Surely, only the barest minimum. He was - he lived and died - a man of the most heroic faith. He knew that Jesus was the Messiah. He knew that He was "the Lamb of God." More than this we cannot say.

"Are You He who is to come, or should we look for another?" It was not a doubt, and Jesus did not censure it as a doubt. It was a simple and candid, frank and straightforward question. Jesus replied, "Blessed is the man who does not lose confidence in me." That was all John wanted to hear, a simple confirmation of his suffering faith. He would go to death in confidence and peace.

He was the lamp pointing out the Light. He was a man sent from God to bear witness to the Light. Yet his own personal life was lived largely in the darkness of faith. He knew that Jesus was the Messiah, the Lamb of God who would somehow take away all the world's sin - but that was absolutely all he knew.

He knew that he himself was "preparing the way of the Lord," but all that that meant he did not know.

Yet he went on in obedience and faith, preaching his baptism of repentance. He baptized even Jesus Himself, and hardly knew what he was doing, except that he was obeying the will of God.

He knew the moral law and practiced it perfectly before he preached it. He rebuked Herod, not only for his shameless adultery, but also for all his other misdeeds. He was a fearless man, no matter how much it might cost him. And it cost him a lot.

He was the greatest of the prophets and more than a prophet, the forerunner of God's Anointed. He was to bring his people "knowledge of salvation," knowledge of the Savior.

+

John was hard on the self-righteous Pharisees, but gentle with the poor prostitutes. Everyone, all Jerusalem and Judea, had come out to him. He was a religious phenomenon. He was authentic. He was true. His voice and his example, his teaching and his life, were powerful.

He had been filled with the Holy Spirit from his mother's womb, from his first meeting with Jesus and Mary - and this same Holy Spirit had continued to take ever greater control of this magnificent soul. He had been "in the desert, until the time of his manifestation to Israel."

The desert had taught him and trained him and had made him strong and genuine. He was wise with "the wisdom of truth." He was filled with the grace of God, and as the greatest of God's spokesmen uttered words of authority that the religious rulers might question and object to and oppose, but knew that they had to accept in the end. For more than any mere prophet, he practiced perfectly what he preached before the words passed his lips.

John's conscience had become a new law for Israel. He spoke, and the crowds obeyed submissively. They saw that both he and his words were real.

In the concrete he was not so terribly demanding - "Whoever has two tunics should share with him who has none." It was simple justice. The real demand was for submission and a basic change of heart, a return to God from the carelessness of everyday living. John was preaching a return to genuine religion.

Yet John clashed far more with Herod than the Pharisees. The latter would agree against Jesus that John's disciples fasted just as they did. Therefore, why didn't Jesus' disciples fast? Herod was powerful enough to murder John. But the devil would need more subtle instruments to murder Jesus. John defended the moral law as such. Jesus would die in defense of religious personalism. Jesus would die defending the highest of the moral virtues, the virtue of religion. John died for the lowest, for the virtue of chastity, a part of the lowly virtue of temperance.

Yet John's ethic, his moral achievement, his ringing words, went as far as merely human ethics can go. It took a God-Man to defend the true worship of God. Even Mary and Joseph, with their morality that far surpassed John's in sublimity, did not preach except by example. They obeyed and were silent.

John spoke out to the extent of his gift. Jesus spoke out against the religious authority itself for refusing to accept Himself as the fulfillment of the Law. John castigated the hypocrisy of the Pharisees, but they knew he would not try to replace them. On the other hand, they could see that Jesus was a threat to their very being as the religious leaders of Israel. John pointed out the Messiah. Jesus was the Messiah. The Pharisees were not really threatened by John. But they sensed that if they didn't put an end to Jesus, He would put an end to all the power and security in which they trusted.

John could not do what God alone could do. But he could prepare the way. And that was a job big enough.

+

John was such a threat to Herod that he finally sent men to take him by force and imprison him. The Gospel says that he would send for him in the prison and talk to him and do good things on his advice. John was an influence for good on this spineless Herod. Herod was afraid of him, but found pleasure in talking to him.

Herodias observed all this and didn't like it. It had been hard enough for her to get Herod to imprison John, but she had finally succeeded. If she wasn't careful, John the prisoner could become more dangerous than John freely preaching and baptizing.

We all know the disgusting story of her and her daughter - and of the culmination of Herod's spinelessness. The story of John's murder is one of the blackest of all human tales. Only the plain words of the Gospel are able to present it adequately in all its abysmal baseness.

It is a story of the bottomless depths to which human corruption can sink when it is confronted by and rejects "the splendor of truth." The pagan world can joke about John, because to all appearances there was not the least trace of glory in his death. John lived absolutely for Another World. And he could not see it. It was a Better World. It was - it is - a World of Light and Sunshine, and he entered it from the malodorous darkness of a dungeon.

The story of John's death is a study in contrasts. The man of sterling faith is destroyed by two dissolute women and their totally corrupted slave of lust. The man of utter integrity goes to his death in apparently sorry isolation, while under the same roof a lascivious party gets increased entertainment from his martyrdom.

John was a man of steel, a man of iron, a man of God. His greatness is almost hidden from us by all our compromises with the world. We are so used to expecting rewards for our virtue in this life. We are so used to judging values by their material sparkle. We are so used to accepting the way of the world and living at least to some extent by our senses.

It takes a very pure heart to really see and appreciate the glory of John. While he was "a lamp burning and shining," he was obviously magnificent. Preaching fearlessly and baptizing boldly for the honor of God, he was a vision splendid to behold.

But when the powers of this world had apparently overcome and silenced him, perhaps even crushed and humbled him, at least as far as things went on the surface, it quickly became another story. Heroes who don't visibly triumph with success in this world, here and now, have never been and never will be the really popular heroes. John's sublimity was of another and transcendent order. He belongs to the Church of God and the Kingdom of Heaven.

+

It is not easy to finish talking about the greatness of John the Baptizer. He was alone. All his life he was alone. His greatness condemned him to a unique solitude. But that very greatness kept him from wallowing in loneliness.

He had a job to do, and not many years in which to do it. The good die young, and he was to die even younger than Jesus. His virtues of truthfulness and chastity were his strength and his transcendent obedience. He knew that he was sent from God, sent by God, to bring the old order to an end by introducing the new. He knew enough, but no more than was necessary. He knew only what he had to do, but he knew that thoroughly. His real power was his knowledge of what God wanted, his conviction of what God wanted him to do.

He was fearless because the truth gave him power. Grace and truth had kept him always free from passion and pride. As a boy even, he had quickly grown very strong and very wise. He knew human beings, as only one who observes them silently can know them. He knew all the petty lies of which the human heart is capable. He knew the basic, deep-down, hidden cowardice of the "powerful."

He knew all the ways of the world to which he was speaking. He knew human weakness as one who had never succumbed to it, never denied the light, never turned from the good to do evil. He knew human malice as one who could see, as one whose eyes had been trained by the solitude of the desert to discern the diabolical. He had fought the devil and won a far greater victory than Anthony of Egypt would.

John was a great miracle of divine grace. He was human nature the way God wanted it to be. He was pure truth and virtue that were not ashamed of themselves, that had passed beyond self-consciousness to utter absorption in the objective purity of things, in the objective order of plain reality.

John was as un-self-conscious as anyone can be. Deep in his heart there burned a love for God that was all devotion to his task and fidelity to the way of faith that he knew he had to walk. He would walk this way of pure faith to the very end, never faltering, never falling. His question to Jesus was a prayer. And Jesus treated it as such. "Blessed is the man who does not lose confidence in me." He was saying, "Blessed are you, John. Remain faithful."

+

We must come to an end of our contemplation of the great John the Baptizer. We must move on to the rest of the story of Jesus, to the development of the total drama. We have dwelt long on him because his life and death, his glorious virtue and apparent defeat, are the introduction to and the pattern of those of Jesus Himself.

John excoriated the Pharisees. Jesus would do the same with far more power and perseverance. John rebuked Herod. Jesus, in passing, labeled Herod as the "fox" that he was and let him know that He would go on preaching and healing until it suited Him to end His work. Herod retaliated against John, but against Jesus he hardly managed to become more than a boor, not even meriting a single word of reply when Pilate would send Him on to him.

John's earthly career, after it had run its course, was brought to an end by the earthly power of Herod. Jesus' longer career, when His "hour" had finally come, was brought to an end by Judas, the Pharisees, the Sadducees, the Scribes, the Lawyers, and the devil, all using Pontius Pilate. John's story was that of Jesus in miniature.

On a far grander scale than John's, the splendid triumph of Jesus would pass through a defeat more public and sensational than John's, yet in the same magnificent tradition of truthfulness. Both murders were examples of the profound evil of which man is capable when he chooses it with open eyes.

John's final strength was the word of Jesus to him. Jesus in His turn, the Son of God, would lean on the strength of God. John and Jesus were both men. John needed Jesus to confirm him in his terrible journey of faith. The Human Heart of Jesus needed the Strength of God in the person of the angel sent to sustain Him in His agony and enable Him to move forward to the Way of the Cross and Crucifixion.

Jesus, the God-Man, has given us John to point out to us the rigors of fidelity to the end, and by his perfect example to obtain for us the grace to do likewise on our infinitely smaller scale. The lesson we learn from John is the lesson of adding prayer to our struggling but perhaps heroic faith. "Are You He. ..?" The answer comes, "Confidence!"

III

Jesus, the Son of Joseph of Nazareth

John had said, "There is the Lamb of God!" And Andrew and that other John who was to become the Apostle had followed Jesus.

"Jesus turned round, and seeing them following Him, said to them, 'What is it you seek?' They said to Him, 'Master, where do You live?' He said to them, 'Come and see.'"

And the Gospel says that they did come, "and saw where He was staying," and stayed with Him the rest of that day, from about four in the afternoon.

After that Andrew found his brother, Simon, and told him, "We have found the Messiah," and brought him to Jesus. Jesus looked at him and said, "You are Simon, the son of John. You shall be called Peter."

The next day Jesus was about to leave Judea for Galilee, and found Philip. He said to Philip, "Follow me." Andrew, Peter and Philip were all from Bethsaida in Galilee.

Then the Gospel says, "Philip found Nathanael, and said to him, 'We have found Him of whom Moses wrote in the Law and the Prophets, Jesus, the Son of Joseph of

Nazareth.' Nathanael said to him, 'Can anything good come out of Nazareth?' Philip said to him, 'Come and see.'"

The Gospel goes on, "Jesus saw Nathanael coming to Him and said of him, 'There's a real Israelite in whom there is no guile.'

"Nathanael said to Him, 'How do You know me?' Jesus answered, 'Before Philip called you, when you were under the fig tree, I saw you.' Nathanael said, 'Master, You are the Son of God! You are the King of Israel!'"

Jesus said to him, "You believe because I told you I saw you under the fig tree. You shall see greater things than that."

The next day they all arrived at Cana in Galilee, where Jesus had been headed. His Mother, Mary, had been invited to a wedding there, and Jesus for her sake, and His followers were welcomed for His sake.

It happened that the bride and groom ran out of wine. Mary remarked it to Jesus. He said to her, "What's that got to do with you and me, Woman? My hour has not yet come." Then she told the attendants, "Do whatever He tells you."

The evangelist tells us that there were six big water jars there. Jesus said to the attendants, "Fill the jars with water." They filled them to the brim. Then He said, "Draw some out now, and take it to the master of the feast." They did so.

When the man had tasted the water "after it had become wine," not knowing that it had been water, though the attendants knew, he called the bridegroom over and said to him, "Every man at first sets out the good wine, then when everyone has drunk freely, the poorer. But you have kept the good wine until now."

John the Evangelist says that by this first of His "signs" Jesus "manifested His glory," and His disciples believed in Him.

+

At this point let us stop and reflect for just a moment on this faith, especially as it lived in the Heart of Mary, whom Jesus had left behind at Nazareth perhaps two months before.

The disciples had known Jesus only for a few days and were dumbfounded at the miracle. Mary had known Jesus intimately for thirty years and had practically asked Him for it.

For her it was an entirely unexpected joy. The heart had gone completely out of her when Jesus had left her two months before. And perhaps she sensed that the precious gift of this wonderful closeness at Cana would be her last, until the tragic union on Calvary, and then the ultimate joy of His Resurrection appearance to her.

Perhaps her faith sensed that from now on she would be left behind with their obtuse relatives. After this ecstatic gift of Jesus to her, there would be only the gift of suffering with Him. The crowds would need Him, and soon He would be given up to them completely, and Mary would be left to her life of pain and prayer for the success of His work.

One more time, with His other relatives, she would try to come to Him. And His mission would force Him to proclaim that His mother and brother and sister were everyone who did the will of His Heavenly Father. Mary's' mission was to do that will with the sublimest of all human heroisms in the solitude of an absolutely Perfect Mother, looking on in quiet distress from an obedient distance.

After this first miracle at Cana, Jesus and His Mother Mary, "and His relatives and His disciples," would all go "down to Capernaum" and stay there a few days. But from then on the evangelists will usually separate His "disciples," who followed Him closely, from His unbelieving "relatives," who followed ambiguously from a distance, and with whom Mary, His Mother and His greatest Disciple, was forced by circumstances to remain behind, until she once again draws near at Calvary.

+

"Now the Passover of the Jews was at hand," St. John says, "and Jesus went up to Jerusalem." When He got there, He found there in the Temple "men selling oxen, sheep and doves, and money-changers at their tables." He was roused. He made a kind of whip of cords and began driving them all out of the Temple - the men themselves and the sheep and the oxen, "and He poured out the money" and "overturned the tables." To those who were selling the doves He was gentler. He simply said, "Take these things away, and don't make my Father's House a house of business."

His disciples, as they looked on, thought of that verse of Scripture, "Zeal for Your House has eaten me up!"

But the Jews came up to Him protesting, "What sign can You show us for doing this?" In answer Jesus said to them, "Destroy this Temple, and in three days I will raise it up." They pretended not to understand that He was speaking of the Temple of His Body and obstinately referred His words instead to the building that had taken 46 years to construct.

Thus began the warfare between Jesus and the religious leaders of His people, the drama, that would end only in His crucifixion and death. For on the deeper level He was not warring "against flesh and blood." It was war with the devil that Jesus had come into this world to wage. He had come "to destroy the works of the devil," and He was beginning here in His Father's House.

St. John remarks that when Jesus had risen victorious from the dead, His disciples would remember these first prophetic words of His.

+

Jesus' exhibition of power in the Temple in Jerusalem at Passover time caused many people to believe in Him. One of these was the Pharisee, Nicodemus. This man came to Jesus, cautiously, by night, and in their conversation said to Him, "Master, we know that You have come as a Teacher from God, for no one could do the things You do unless God were with him."

Jesus said to him, "I tell you solemnly, unless a person be born again, he cannot see the Kingdom of God."

Nicodemus was perplexed. "How can a man be born when he's old? Can he enter his mother's womb a second time and be born again?"

Jesus said, "I tell you solemnly, unless a person be born again of water and the Holy Spirit, he cannot enter the

Kingdom of God. What is born of the flesh is flesh. What is born of the Spirit is spirit."

Nicodemus said, "How can such things be?"

Jesus said, "You're a teacher in Israel and don't know these things? I tell you solemnly, we speak of what we know and bear witness to what we have seen, and our witness you do not receive."

Jesus went on, "No one has ascended into Heaven except Him who has descended from Heaven, the Son of Man....And as Moses lifted up the serpent in the desert, even so must the Son of Man be lifted up, that those who believe in Him may not be lost, but may have eternal life."

Then either Jesus or St. John continues, "For God so loved the world that He gave His only Son, that whoever believes in Him may not be lost, but may have eternal life."

+

After this Jesus would stay south for awhile in Judea, baptizing people through the instrumentality of His disciples. The Gospel says that John the Baptizer "was also baptizing in Aennon, near Salim, for there was a lot of water there."

John's disciples told him that Jesus was baptizing and that crowds were coming to Him. John answered that he was not the Messiah but had been sent before Him. "He who has the Bride is the Bridegroom. The friend of the Bridegroom....rejoices greatly at the voice of the Bridegroom. This is my joy....and it is complete. He must increase. I must decrease."

But when Jesus found out that the Pharisees had heard

that He was making and baptizing even more disciples than John, He decided to leave Judea and go again into Galilee.

He had to pass through Samaria, and we all know the beautiful story of His encounter with the Samaritan woman at Jacob's well.

After that, when He arrived in Galilee, the people there welcomed Him, because - like Nicodemus - they had been at the Passover Feast in Jerusalem and had witnessed all He had done there in the Temple during the Feast.

He went first back to Cana, where He had turned the water into wine. There was a government official there whose son was sick in Capernaum. He had come to ask Jesus to go to Capernaum and heal his son, who was about to die.

Jesus said to him, "Unless you people see signs and wonders, you don't believe." The official pleaded, "Sir, come with me before my child dies!" Jesus said to him, "Go your way. Your son will live."

The man believed Jesus' words and left. On his way home his servants met him on the road with the news that his son was going to live. He asked them what time it was when his son had got better, and they said, "It was one o'clock yesterday afternoon when the fever left him." The father remembered, then, that it was at that very hour that Jesus had told him, "Your son will live." The Gospel says that he and his whole household believed.

St. John remarks that "this was a second sign that Jesus worked when coming from Judea into Galilee." And perhaps we should add that there do not yet seem to have been any miracles at all in Jerusalem, nor throughout the whole of Jesus' public life would there be but a relatively few miracles down south in Jerusalem and Judea, whereas up north in Galilee they were to be utterly beyond counting.

+

Jesus left Cana and went to Nazareth where He had been brought up, and on the Sabbath Day He went as usual to the synagogue. He stood up to read the Scriptures, and was handed the book of the prophet Isaiah. He unrolled the scroll and found the place where it is written, "The Spirit of the Lord is upon me. He has sent me to preach good news to the poor, to proclaim liberty to captives and sight to the blind, to set free the oppressed, and announce the year when the Lord will save His people."

Jesus rolled up the scroll, gave it back to the attendant, and sat down. Everyone in the synagogue had his eyes fixed on Him. He began speaking to them. "This passage of Scripture has been fulfilled today, as you heard it being read." They spoke favorably of Him to one another and marvelled at how appealing His speech was. They remarked, "Isn't this Joseph's son?" They approved of Him.

But then Jesus said to them, "You will doubtless quote me the proverb, 'Physician, heal yourself,' and say, 'Do here in your own home town such things as we were told happened in Capernaum. Nazareth had heard of Jesus' healing of the government official's son there while He was in Cana. He went on, "I tell you this, a prophet is never accepted in his own home town. Listen to me. There were many widows in Israel in the days of Elijah, when there was no rain for three and a half years, and a great famine spread over the land. Yet Elijah was not sent to a single one of them, but only to a widow of Zarephath, near Sidon. And there were many lepers in Israel during the time of Elisha. Yet not one of them was cured, but only Naaman the Syrian."

At this everyone in the synagogue was filled with anger. They rose up, dragged Jesus out of the town, and took Him to the top of the hill on which it was built, to throw Him over the cliff.

But St. Luke says He walked through the middle of the crowd and went His way.

+

He left Nazareth and went to Capernaum. From that time on He began to preach, "Repent! The Kingdom of Heaven is at hand!"

News of Him quickly began to spread throughout the whole region. "He taught in their synagogues," and all the people held Him in honor.

He taught the people on the Sabbath, and they were spellbound, because His words had authority.

He went all over Galilee, preaching the Good News of the Kingdom of God and healing people of every kind of disease and sickness. He had come back to Galilee from Jerusalem "with the power of the Spirit on Him," and word was spreading through all the neighboring country, even throughout "the whole region of Syria," so that people brought Him all those who were sick with all kinds of diseases, and afflicted with all sorts of troubles - people with demons, epileptics, paralytics. Jesus healed them all. Great crowds followed Him from all of Galilee and the region of "the Ten Cities," from Jerusalem and Judea and the area east of the Jordan.

Jesus could no longer openly enter a town, but remained outside in lonely places. Yet people kept coming to Him from all sides. Still, He would manage to get away and pray in solitude.

But He healed people wherever they were, wherever He met them - even on the Sabbath. At this last "breach of the Law" the Pharisees were outraged. Finally, after one particularly bold cure by Jesus, in the synagogue itself and on a Sabbath, they became "filled with fury," and began to discuss among themselves what they should do to Him. They left the synagogue and met at once with some members of Herod's party and made plans to kill Him.

+

It was the beginning. Jesus had chosen Andrew and John, Peter and James, Philip and Nathanael, and later Matthew. He had first healed Peter's mother-in-law at their home in Capernaum of a bad fever. That miracle had set off a day of them that lasted far into the evening.

When the people of Capernaum had sought Him out again the next morning - Peter said, "Everybody's looking for You!" - Jesus had replied that He had to move on to the other towns, for that was why He had come.

And move He did. He began to move and to act - *facere et docere*, "to do and to teach."

He had begun to preach and teach and heal, and the people, tremendous crowds, were flocking to Him and responding enthusiastically.

It was a triumphant beginning. But already the shadows had begun to appear. Already the Pharisees were opposing Him. Already there was hatred, hatred of the Truth. Already there was war.

It would go on for more than two full years, the clashes the sparks. Jesus would declare Himself, time after time, and the Pharisees would repeatedly reject Him.

The people, the crowds, all seemed to be in love with Jesus. But "He knew what was in man." He knew how shallow was this devotion, generally speaking. Yet He accepted it patiently. He would not crush the bruised reed nor snuff out the smoldering wick. He knew the human heart, but not only in its treacherousness, in its abysmal weakness and poverty as well. The people needed Him. For this had He come.

Their bodies, minds, souls, hearts needed Him, needed to be healed. The throngs, the human masses, needed the truth and love that only He could provide. Man is above all poor. And God is rich, "rich in mercy" and in everything else. Man needs God. Jesus was the Savior.

"Power went out from Him and healed everyone." Truth went out from Him and healed minds. Love went out from Him and healed hearts.

It was indeed a wonderful thing, this passing of Jesus Christ up and down the hills and roads of Galilee, scattering graces of strength and joy. It was blissful. It was ecstatic. It was truly "God among us."

Jesus did not blame the poor people for their shallowness. He was the Personification of Patience. Even us who know better He does not condemn. He simply waits. He awaits our conversion.

He was gentle, and He prayed. He would always manage to get away and be with His Father in prayer, at least during the nights, when everyone else slept for sheer fatigue.

He too was fatigued, but sometimes His soul needed prayer more than His body needed sleep. And so He prayed, spent the night in prayer - *pernoctans in oratione Dei.* He prayed the prayer of God.

But during all the daylight hours He was available, to the sheep that needed their Shepherd. And His availability has passed into the Eucharist, for our sakes, an availability that stretches into and all through the nights. He is "God with us."

We need Him. The crowds needed Him 2,000 years ago, and we need Him today. Blessed is the religious house where Jesus Christ lives in the tabernacle, under the one roof, and is available on sleepless nights. Blessed be Jesus Christ in the Most Holy Sacrament of the Altar.

Blessed be Jesus Christ, who looked down from His Heavenly Throne and saw the millions and billions of us poor struggling sinners, and in the darkness of the night leapt down to be with us, to walk among us and bring us security and peace, salvation and holiness, in His own loving Presence.

+

It was a joy for the people to follow Him. It was not physically easy. He kept moving. He demanded much. The soul came first. Yet the crowds followed, even forgetful that they were in need of food for their bodies, so happy were they to have their souls being fed abundantly.

Nothing like this had ever been known in Israel, or truly in all the world. They were glorious days, blessed days, the days of Christ's historical presence in our world. And if we will to have it so, by faith, they are Eucharistically prolonged, and we have only to approach Him present in our churches in this Sacrament. He is as truly with us as He ever was, in fact, more truly now that His Holy Spirit has come at Pentecost for all the ensuing ages.

The crowds loved Him, in their way, but "the Holy Spirit had not yet been given," and they didn't really know quite what - or whom - they loved. A prophet? The Messiah?

The God-Man. We know it, but they did not see it so clearly. Peter and the Apostles had inklings - "the Son of the Living God" - but even they perhaps did not yet fully understand all that that meant. It was genuine faith, but perhaps considerably more obscure than it would later be.

Yet even if the crowds did not know exactly what they believed, still they followed. He thrilled them, thrilled their hearts, the hearts of the poor. Once again, we have to repeat that He did not blame them for not all being saints. He was the Lord, "kind and merciful." He was teaching, leading, slowly.

It was good to follow Him as He moved along. There was peace and prayer in His footsteps. There was a calm and quiet happiness. It was good to be with Him. It was choosing "the better part," even to the forgetfulness of other things that needed to be done, but as it turned out, could be done later.

He Himself was "the One Thing Necessary," and it was good to be there with Him in the road, going wherever He was going, secure in the knowledge that He knew, and that was enough. He was "the good Jesus," and the people knew instinctively that He could not lead them, even following blindly as they did, anywhere except to blessedness.

And so they followed, and continued to follow, up and down the roads, up and over the hills, wherever He led. He was leading them to Himself, the Truth, and to His Father, "the God of all consolation." He was giving them the encouragement they needed to believe in prayer.

+

He was no Pied Piper, and yet they were children, joyfully following Him. And we are children, when we have the humility and faith to abandon all and follow Him as they did.

They did well to follow Him, and so do we. They were fascinated by "signs and wonders" and loaves of bread that contented their hunger. And we, even after Pentecost, are not always so terribly different. We remain little children, attracted by all that sparkles and glitters, by the sensational, the extraordinary, even in the realms of prayer and faith, even in the realm of religion.

And yet we are children, and we do well to follow Him any way we can. If only we follow, He will transform our childishness into solid virtue in His own good time. He will transform our undependable "devotion" into true and real and perfect religion, even into heroic faith.

He will transform us - into Himself, and we will be able to say, "I live, now no longer I, the sick man, but Jesus Christ lives in me, the Whole Man."

He will lead us in the way of transformation, and He will transform it into the way of perfect love.

"This is the victory" of love and peace, "our faith." It is not yet the perfect and absolute victory of the enjoyment of the Beatific Vision in the Kingdom of Heaven, "new heavens and a new earth," but it is nevertheless real victory.

Jesus Christ is leading us, just as truly as He led the crowds, the throngs, along the roads of Galilee. We need the picture, the imagery, that the Gospels give us of "this Jesus," leading, moving forward to Jerusalem, to Calvary, to crucifixion and death, but also and ultimately to Resurrection and Eternally Triumphant Life.

We need the joy of contemplating all the things that He did so "gloriously." We need the thrill of knowing that He is God and has come among us and will never leave us again. He left this world at His Ascension, but only for ten days, and only to return at the first Pentecost more powerful than ever in His wonderful Holy Spirit. And now He remains with us in this Gift of God, having become for us Himself the Source of Infinite Energy and Hope as our "Lifegiving Spirit."

"The Lord is the Spirit." He is the Spirit of Truth and Life and Love. "God is a Spirit, and those who worship Him must worship Him in spirit and in truth." The Father, the Son and the Holy Spirit are "one Spirit," and when we are "joined to the Lord," we too become "one spirit" with the Triune God.

"Where the Spirit of the Lord is, there is freedom."

Wherever Jesus passed, in Galilee or even in Judea, there was glorious freedom. The Pharisees might hound Him, but He would rebuke them roundly, to the delight of the common people. The evangelists say that these poor "hung on His words."

Blessed are we when we read the Gospels and share in this thrilling joy that Jesus Christ gives to the poor, the common people. But sometimes we may read the Gospels and find ourselves rebuked as Pharisees. It is so. We are not perfect, perhaps far from it. But we know that Jesus says to the lukewarm in the Book of Revelation, "It is those I love that I chasten," and we accept the correction and are humbled. "The words of the Word" purify our sinful hearts.

But like Peter, we come back for more, knowing that somehow, in the end, God's all powerful grace will have its way with us. We know that we are cowardly sinners. But we also know what's good for us.

We know that there is simply no place else to go. Jesus Christ, and only He, has everything we need - and we need correction. But His words - we know it in faith - are the words of a Lover, the Truest of all lovers. We know it by faith even when we don't feel it.

We believe in His love for us. And this is our victory. He would one day say, "In the world you will have distress. But confidence! I have overcome the world!"

We are aware that "the world" is very much alive in us. We are still, even perhaps after many years of following Jesus Christ, largely pagans. But we refuse to quit. We refuse to give up. For we have experienced that even in His chastisements, and perhaps especially there, "this Jesus" is a God of Peace and has won for us the Victory of Peace.

And so we keep on following, in pure, unfeeling faith. He is a "hard Man" only on the surface. In reality He loves us profoundly and wants us with Him forever in perfect joy in the Heavenly Kingdom of His Father. He is training us to be victorious in the battle against the devil, who would divert our free will to hell. We know that Jesus Christ loves us more than we will ever be able to conceive. We know "in whom we have believed."

IV

The Lilies of the Field

St. John says that the Jews “kept persecuting Jesus” for healing people on the Sabbath. But Jesus answered them, “My Father works even until now, and I work.” And this was why they were seeking even more “to put Him to death - because He was not only breaking the Sabbath, but was also calling God His Father, thereby making Himself equal to God.”

Jesus told them that John the Baptizer “was the lamp, burning and shining,” and that they “desired to rejoice for awhile in his light.” But He declared that the witness that He Himself had was greater than that of John. “For the works that the Father has given me to accomplish, these very works that I do bear witness to me, that the Father has sent me. And the Father Himself, who has sent me, has borne witness to me, but you have never heard His voice or seen His Face, and you do not have His word abiding in you, since you do not believe Him whom He has sent.”

His disciples couldn’t even pluck a few ears of corn and husk them to eat, when they were walking through the standing grain on the Sabbath, without the ever watchful Pharisees pouting and complaining, “Your disciples are doing what is not lawful for them to do on the Sabbath."

Jesus told them how David and his men had even eaten the loaves of bread set out in the Temple when they were hungry and needed them, when only the priests could eat them lawfully, and how on the Sabbath days the priests themselves break the Sabbath in the Temple without guilt. And He said to them, "But I tell you that One greater than the Temple is here. But if you knew what this means, 'I desire mercy and not sacrifice,' you would never have condemned the innocent."

He concluded, "The Sabbath was made for man, not man for the Sabbath," and told them, "The Son of Man is Lord even of the Sabbath."

The crowds kept following Him - from all of Galilee and Judea, from Jerusalem and Idumea, and from the other side of the Jordan, even from as far away as Tyre and Sidon on the coast of the Mediterranean.

+

Then one day early in the summer Jesus went out to a mountain to pray and spent the whole night "in the prayer of God." At daybreak He called His disciples together and selected twelve of them to be His Apostles: Simon, to whom He gave the name Peter, and Andrew his brother, James and John, Philip and Bartholomew (or Nathanael), Matthew and Thomas, James the son of Alphaeus and Simon called the Zealot, Judas the son of James, and Judas Iscariot, "who turned traitor."

Coming down the mountain with them, He stopped at a level stretch where there was a large crowd of His disciples who had come to hear Him and be healed of their diseases. The whole crowd was trying to touch Him, because "power went out from Him and healed them all."

He sat down, let them quiet down and gather around Him, and began to teach them:

"Blessed are the poor in spirit, for theirs is the Kingdom of Heaven. Blessed are they who mourn, for they shall be comforted. Blessed are the meek, for they shall possess the land. Blessed are they who hunger and thirst for justice, for they shall be satisfied. Blessed are the merciful, for they shall obtain mercy. Blessed are the pure of heart, for they shall see God. Blessed are the peacemakers, for they shall be called the children of God. Blessed are they who suffer persecution for justice' sake, for theirs is the Kingdom of Heaven.

"Blessed are you, when men reproach you and persecute you, and speaking falsely, say all manner of evil against you, for my sake. Rejoice and exult, for your reward is great in Heaven. For so did they persecute the prophets who were before you....

"You are the salt of the earth.... You are the light of the world....

"You have heard that it was said, 'You shall love your neighbor and hate your enemy.' But I say to you who are listening, Love your enemies, do good to those who hate you. Bless those who curse you, pray for those who calumniate you, that you may be children of your Father in Heaven, who makes His sun rise on the just and the unjust.

"And even as you wish people to do to you, so also you do to them....

"In praying do not multiply words.... Pray like this: Our

Father, who art in Heaven, hallowed be Thy name. Thy Kingdom come. Thy will be done, on earth as it is in Heaven. Give us this day our daily bread, and forgive us our trespasses, as we forgive those who trespass against us. And lead us not into temptation, but deliver us from evil.

"Do not lay up for yourselves treasures on earth, where rust and moth consume, and where thieves break in and steal. But lay up for yourselves treasures in Heaven, where neither rust nor moth consumes, nor thieves break in and steal. For where your treasure is, there will your heart be also....

"Look at the birds of the air. They neither sow nor reap nor gather into barns. Yet your Heavenly Father feeds them. Are not you of much more value than they? Which of you by worrying can add a moment to his life-span?

"And as for clothing, why are you anxious? See how the lilies of the field grow. They neither toil nor spin. Yet I assure you, not even Solomon in all his glory was arrayed like one of these. But if God so clothes the grass of the field, which today is alive and tomorrow is thrown into the oven, how much more you, O you of little faith!

"Therefore do not be anxious, and say, 'What shall we eat?' or 'What shall we put on?' for after all these things the unbelievers seek. For your Father knows that you need all these things. But seek first the Kingdom of God and His justice, and all these things shall be given you besides. Therefore do not be anxious about tomorrow, for tomorrow will have anxieties of its own. Sufficient for the day is the evil thereof.

"Do not judge, and you shall not be judged. Do not condemn, and you shall not be condemned. Your verdict on others will be the verdict passed on you. Forgive, and you shall be forgiven. Give, and it shall be given to you. Good measure, pressed down, shaken together, running over, shall they pour into your lap. The measure with which you measure will be measured back to you.

"Ask, and you shall receive. Seek, and you shall find. Knock, and the door will be opened to you. For everyone who asks receives, and whoever seeks finds, and to the one who knocks the door will be opened. Or what man is there among you who, if his son asks him for a loaf of bread, will hand him a stone? Or if he asks for a fish, will hand him a snake? Or if he asks for an egg, will hand him a scorpion? If you, then, evil as you are, know how to give good gifts to your children, how much more will your Heavenly Father give His Holy Spirit to those who ask Him!...."

When Jesus had finished speaking, the crowds were spellbound at His teaching. The reason was that He taught with authority, "and not like their scribes."

+

Jesus' words in this famous Sermon on the Mount were words of joy. He was always a wonder, wherever He went and whatever He did. He would come down from the mountain after finishing His long sermon, and heal a centurion's servant, marvelling at this Gentile's faith, and declaring that many would come from the east and the west to feast "with Abraham, Isaac and Jacob in the Kingdom of Heaven," while the children of the Kingdom themselves would be put out into "the exterior darkness."

He would go on a little later and raise to life the dead

son of a widow in the little town of Naim, and with love and happiness give him back to his mother.

He would praise John the Baptizer and chide the generation for its utter inconsistency in declaring John was possessed by the devil, since he neither ate bread nor drank wine, but that Jesus Himself was both a glutton and addicted to wine because He ate and drank in friendship with poor sinners.

He would gratefully accept the love of Mary Magdalen, and send her away sinless and blissful. To her He would simply say, "Your faith has saved you. Go in peace." To this magnificent human heart He did not need to add, "and from now on sin no more," as He did with other lesser souls.

Then St. Luke says that He was continuing to journey "through towns and villages, preaching and proclaiming the Good News of the Kingdom of God. And with Him were the Twelve, and certain women who had been cured of evil spirits and infirmities - Mary, who is called the Magdalene, from whom seven devils had gone out, and Joanna, the wife of Chuza, Herod's steward, and Susanna, and many others, who used to provide for them out of their means."

The crowds so carried Jesus along that His relatives actually thought He had gone crazy. Yet He would calmly cure a possessed man who was both blind and mute, and when the Pharisees would refuse to accept it and say that He did it by diabolical power, Jesus would warn them that any other sin would be forgiven them, but not blasphemy against the Holy Spirit.

Then His relatives would try once again to get near Him, and Mary His Mother would be with them of necessity, and Jesus, "stretching forth His hand to His disciples," would speak these words so austerely wonderful, "Here are my mother and my brothers! Whoever does the will of my Father in Heaven, he is my brother and sister and mother."

And Mary, who was doing that will to the uttermost Perfection, would go on in the darkness of faith and suffering, supporting Him from a distance by her unconditional devotion, submitting heroically without understanding, and in doing so teaching us all to live by sheer faith in this utterly Mysterious and Holy God.

+

Jesus would point to "the lilies of the field" and say to all, "See how they grow!" And His own life would be an ongoing lesson in this freedom of the children of God. "Look at the birds of the air. They neither sow nor reap nor gather into barns. Yet your Heavenly Father feeds them." It is true that "They have to pick it up!" And they have to work hard going around and searching it out. But they don't worry. They just do it.

Jesus worked hard, day in and day out, always at the disposal of huge, unthinking crowds - always kind, always merciful, always patient. It was a wonderful thing. He was one with the lilies of the field and the birds of the air. He was free. He was the Truth who was bringing freedom into a world that had been for many long ages enslaved to sin and to the fear of death and to the devil.

He kept moving, not always, but usually. In the beginning He had preached in the synagogues, even if perhaps to overflow crowds. But now it seems that it was more frequently out in the open that He spoke to great numbers gathered together time after time. The Sermon on the Mount seems to have been perhaps only the first of many similar sermons, similarly patterned, all over the regions through which He travelled.

He was at home in the fields and along the roads just as much as in the synagogues. He was at home everywhere. He was at home in His Father's world, on His Father's earth, in His people's land. He loved the poor people who followed Him, and their simple, though entirely undependable, devotion gave Him happiness. He knew how utterly poor they were - morally poor, sinful sheep who would just simply destroy themselves forever unless His infinite mercy and patience reached out to them continually, over and over again, even to His physical exhaustion.

He would get exhausted. His limited body would be overcome by fatigue, and He would necessarily fall asleep, even on a cushion in the back of Peter's boat. He would be roused from His utterly necessary rest by their fear of the storm that was raging. And when, after He had calmed it, they reached the other side of the lake, having fled the crowds on the first shore, He would find nothing but more work for Him to do waiting on the second.

He was a wondrous Miracle of Divine and Human Mercy everywhere He went. And He truly went everywhere. His mission was "to the lost sheep of the House of Israel," and it seemed as if He were seeking out geographically every last one of them, all throughout the length and breadth of the land.

It is a beautiful story. He was a beautiful Man.

+

He was a Man who believed in beauty. He was the Man, the Divine Man, who had created the lilies of the field. He loved all the beauties of the fields, the hills, the rolling roads. He loved the towns and villages, and we must be grateful to St. Francis of Assisi for giving us "the most perfect image" of Him.

He loved "the birds of the air" as Francis would after Him, and far more profoundly. He loved the sparrows as His Father loved them. But really He loved all these things for our sakes. He loved us. It was people, it was us, He loved in all these accoutrements of our universe. He assured us with infinite care and concern that the lilies of the field and the birds of the air only existed to help us to Heaven. All things are signs of the Father's love for us. This is the pure and essential Gospel - that God loves us, infinitely.

The Gospel gets complicated by its expositors. It becomes "the Gospel of this" and "the Gospel of that." But the Gospel in all its truth and simplicity is purely and simply the Good News that God loves us and has sent His Son to speak that love to us by His whole life and death, by His crucifixion sacrifice and His Resurrection victory.

With every word that Jesus spoke, to all the tremendous crowds that followed Him in hope, He was saying, over and over again in a thousand different ways, "The Father Himself loves you! Believe in His love for you!"

Believe! "Only believe!" And your faith will make you whole.

Indeed, there is no obstacle on His part. He is Love and Generosity Personified. But if we refuse to believe and trust, and ask! - even desperately: "Lord, I believe! Help my unbelief!" - that love and generosity cannot reach us.

Yet how poor we are - poor in faith, poor in trust and confidence. "O you of little faith!"

So we read the Gospels. We come back to the Story. We contemplate the Marvel, and we make our "feeble efforts" - and grace has its way. Power goes out from Him, and reaches us, and heals us even of our unbelief and lack of trust and confidence.

Truly we have nothing - nothing but Him. Truly is He "Christ our Hope." Even if He seems to be "a hard man," always demanding more, we know that it is because He loves us, and like an eagle teaching its young to fly, cannot be easy on us. For we must learn to depend on Him heroically or perish as the devil's prey.

+

"Do not be anxious.... But seek first the Kingdom of God and His justice, and all these other things will be given you besides." It is the blueprint for happiness, if only we choose to do it.

And there is only one way to successfully do it, and that is to keep our eyes fixed on "this Jesus." Observe how He practiced what He preached. "The Son of Man has no place to lay His head," except maybe on that famous cushion in the stern of Peter's boat. He had no fixed abode. He lay down at night wherever His Heavenly Father's will had led Him.

He is our Inspiration, and all the Inspiration we need. He is the only really Free Man the world has ever known. He is the Truth, and His Life was all Truth. He would preach to the people, and the crowds would come to Him, and increase, and He would serve them in every conceivable way. Then He would grow humanly exhausted and need to get away and rest and be quiet and pray to His Father in solitude. Then the crowds would find Him out in His hideaway, and He would have compassion on them, "sheep without a shepherd," and go on healing their sick - and healing their minds with the truth and even feeding their bodies with miraculous bread.

"No one who comes to me will I reject." He practiced it to perfection. Mercy and patience were a way of life for Him. He would not stoop to settling petty quarrels - "Man! Who has set me up as judge over you?" - but He never left a real problem unresolved. Absolutely everyone who came to Him with living faith, no matter how poor and struggling, went away healed and wholed.

"Lord, I believe! Help my unbelief!" It is the prayer, the cry of hope, of all of us at some time or other in our lives. "Help my unbelief!" We want to believe, we yearn to believe, we do believe, but we are so weak, so pitiful, so poor in our "feeble efforts."

He knows our frame. He sees our desperate weakness. And he meets us far more than halfway. Our humiliating spiritual poverty draws from Him all the wealth of His power and strength. He says a word, and we are saved and restored to peace and stability.

For it is not really anything He has to give that we need. It is He Himself. We need His goodness. We need to experience that He loves us, that He is Power, that He rules all things. We need to experience that utter confidence in Him is itself our reward, our heart's union with His in peace and love.

It is not surprising that we need Him, for He made us for Himself. He made us to need Him. And indeed, He needs us. His Human Heart needs the love of ours. And that is why He left His Mother's home in Nazareth and set out along the roads, in search of all His Father had given Him to cherish and to save.

+

It is a Mystery - this need of ours for Him, which is one with His need of us. It is a Mystery of Love. As God, of course, He does not need us. But in becoming human, in assuming a human nature like ours "in all things but sin," in taking to Himself a Human Heart like ours, He has chosen to need us as His completion, as a Husband needs His Bride. We are His Church, the fullness of Him who fills the whole universe. We are necessary members of His Body.

He needs us, not only as apostolic instruments by which He wills to save the rest of the world. No, He needs us all as a Lover needs His Beloved. We are His Bride, the Church. We are His brothers and sisters. We are His children, His sheep, His family.

He cannot do without us, unless we finally choose to do without Him. He cannot be happy without us, unless in the end we choose the unadulterated misery of hell. He loves us, as long as we do not finally choose eternal hatred. He waits for us with Divine Patience, as long as we have the humility to hope in His infinite power to do what of ourselves we are powerless to do. He awaits our prayer, and continually showers down on us the graces we need to keep returning to confident communion with Him.

We are dependent. He knows it. We must learn it. We must come to realize it. "Without me you can do nothing." It is not the proud boast of a corrupt tyrant. It is the loving appeal of a God who has given us everything from existence to rationality to a share in His own Divine Nature and Life. It is an appeal to our common sense, to our reason, to our faith, to our hearts.

He is saying, "I love you. I want to give myself to you. Do not reject my love."

He is saying, "Believe in me. I have only gifts to give, of happiness, blessedness, bliss. Believe in my love for you. Trust in me. Come to me, all you who labor and are heavy burdened, and I will give you rest."

He is saying, "Learn of me, for I am meek and humble of heart, and you will find rest for your souls. Pride and self-sufficiency are heavy, loveless burdens. Be my sheep, my child, my friend, and we will walk together in joy and freedom, in truth and love."

He is saying, "Take my yoke upon you, for my yoke is sweet and my burden light. Suffer with me, and you will experience the wonder of a far greater love than is possible in cheap pleasures and the satisfactions of this world. Be with me in prayer, and I will be with you. We will carry the True and Holy Cross together, and the union of our hearts will transform its weight into a foretaste of the Blessedness of my Father's Kingdom, the infinite Blessedness of His Eternal Paradise."

He is saying, "Work with me, labor with me, and together we will bring this happiness to many other human hearts, and the pure joy of the burden of our labors will be multiplied to infinity, in precious human hearts all over the world."

He is saying, "Believe in me, and wait for me, and quickly will I come, to take you to myself. And we shall be together, with all we have loved, unendingly in the Kingdom of Heaven."

+

Christ is our wholeness, and our only wholeness. He is the Model who makes us whole as we contemplate Him by the sheer force of His Divine Personality. It is the power of His human wholeness that goes out to all of us and heals us of all our brokenness and fragmentedness - and gives us joy.

Wholeness is a gift, the peculiar gift - it is almost identical with peace, "Shalom!" - of Jesus to us all. "Your faith has made you whole."

We get it by asking for it. We get it by prayer. "Ask and you shall receive, seek and you shall find...." And then He goes on to tell those two wonderful parables about persistence in prayer. Even if we are lacking in the beautiful humility of the tax collector, and perhaps in the charity or love that goes along with humility, yet if we have the faith to persist in "pestering" this infinitely merciful God, like the poor widow or the importunate friend, we will get what we're after. We will get the Gift of all things in the Gift of the Fullness of the Holy Spirit, or we might say His

Wholeness.

The unjust or "corrupt" judge, who feared neither God nor man, gave way under the persistent complaining of the poor little widow who wanted justice. She was out to survive, and the man was actually afraid that if he didn't come through for her, he'd end up with "a black eye," as the Greek has it.

And the "importunate friend," who comes to his neighbor in the middle of the night and needs bread to set before his guests - does he go away without it? Not on your life! His neighbor says to him, "Don't bother me. We're all in bed. Come back in the morning." And Jesus says, "I tell you the truth, if he won't get up and give to him out of friendship, he will if he keeps pestering him." He'll do anything to get back to sleep. So Jesus says, "I say the same thing to you: Ask! And the gift will come!"

We pray, and we don't get what we want. St. James says it's because God knows we would squander it on our passions. But the answer is to keep on praying, to persist in our begging, as long as necessary, like that precious little widow, like the man who would not take no for an answer - and sooner or later we will get what we are asking for.

For as we persevere in prayer we learn little by little that what we really need to make us happy is simply greater and stronger and more living faith in God's goodness and love for us. There is no lack of the desire to make us happy, even in this world, on God's part. And as we persist in our begging, we come to realize that prayer itself, the prayer of faith, brings the greatest happiness to be found in this world, and the beginning of Heavenly Peace.

Our very persistence brings us peace. We complain to

God, and then are ashamed of ourselves - maybe - but at any rate amazed that we are still alive and in existence. We know that we deserve to be annihilated, and this all good God not only does not punish us for complaining, but actually encourages us to keep on communicating with Him any way we can in ever greater hope, even if it is not always in the most "proper" way and words.

He encourages us to overcome evil with good, to overcome our pride and lack of faith by desperately persisting in demanding true justice from Him. We want to be happy and holy, even sometimes in that order! And He does not send us away rejected. He simply says, "Keep asking! Keep communicating!" And little by little the order reverses itself. Little by little we come to see that prayer itself is the greatest of goods and the only real happiness. And then we begin to pray for holiness first and before all else. We begin to pray for perfect love.

Finally we come to realize the greatness of the tax collector and the good of humility. We may have asked for everything but humility, but in the end God gives us humility, this priceless gift - our very perseverance in prayer has made us humble - and we are at peace in His will for us.

"Ask and you shall receive...." Yet Jesus taught the Apostles to pray not only by giving them words - "Our Father...." - but even more by His own example. He would get apart and be by Himself and spend the night in communion with His Father. "Jesus Himself was in deserted places and in prayer."

Jesus would be deep in prayer, lost in prayer all during the night hours, teaching us that solitude and silence are every bit as productive as active fruitfulness and vitality. In fact there is no genuine spiritual fruitfulness except what one acquires in real contemplation. Unless it is balanced by prayer, the apostolic life degenerates into an "active" life that is all but meaningless - shallow, hollow, even maybe sinful.

But then even in His sacred prayer, the Apostles, urged on by the crowds, would find Him out, and Jesus would make the best of it, and return from the depths of profound recollection to the hectic service of His poor, harried sheep. He would go to them and suffer them, endure them, love them, heal them.

His life was a prayer, a prayer of patience and gentleness, a prayer that every dedicated apostle must learn, through years of humble suffering and fidelity. We must be rooted in prayer. We must be deeply in love with all our hours of prayer, that when the Holy Spirit calls us to leave them for the service of our brothers and sisters it may be truly more prayer that we find in this activity, the prayer of obedience, of true love and true joy.

We pray for fruitfulness and fidelity. We ask for perfect love. And our prayer is transformed into a life poured out in availability to all who need us.

V

The Sower Went Out to Sow His Seed

Jesus was sitting by the Sea of Galilee, and a crowd was gathering around Him. As it grew - people from all the towns around Capernaum - He retreated into a boat moored at the shore, one of the Apostles' boats, most likely Peter's, and sat down there. The crowd stood on the shore and gradually quieted down, in readiness to hear whatever He might say. Then He began His teaching in parables.

"The sower went out to sow his seed, and as he sowed, some seeds fell by the wayside and were trodden underfoot, and the birds came and ate them up. And other seeds fell on rocky ground, where they had not much earth. They sprang up at once, because they had no depth, but when the sun rose they were scorched, and because they had no root they withered away. Other seeds fell among thorns, and the thorns grew up and choked them, and they yielded no fruit. And other seeds fell on good ground and yielded fruit that grew up, increased, and produced, one thirty, another sixty, and another a hundredfold.

Then He said, "Whoever has ears to hear, let him hear."

It was a new way of teaching, and the disciples did not understand it. After the crowds had dispersed, the Apostles asked Jesus about it. He replied that to them, His close and faithful followers, it was given "to know the Mystery of the Kingdom of God," but to the others it was left in parables.

This was because "the heart of this people has been hardened," so that they looked and did not see, listened but did not hear. "With their ears they have become hard of hearing, and their eyes they have closed - lest at any time they see with their eyes and hear with their ears and understand with their mind and be converted, and I heal them."

Then He went on, "But blessed are your eyes, for they see, and your ears, for they hear. For I tell you truly, many prophets and just men have longed to see what you see, and have not seen it, and to hear what you hear, and have not heard it."

He said to them, "You don't understand this parable? How then are you going to understand all the other parables?"

Then He explained. "Listen, then, to the parable of the sower. The sower sows the word. When anyone hears the word of the Kingdom but does not understand it, the evil one comes and snatches away what has been sown in his heart. This is he who was sown by the wayside.

"And the one sown on rocky ground, that is he who hears the word and receives it immediately with joy. Yet he has no root in himself, but continues only for awhile, and when trouble and persecution come because of the word, he at once falls away.

"And the one sown among the thorns, that's the man who listens to the word, but the cares of this world and the deceitfulness of wealth choke the word, and it becomes fruitless.

"And the one sown on good ground, that is he who hears the word and understands it. He bears fruit and yields, in one case a hundredfold, in another sixtyfold, and in another thirtyfold."

It was all so simple - and so profound. It was "the word of the Kingdom." It was the first of the parables, and the pattern of them all. The parables were *par excellence* what St. Augustine called the *verba Verbi*, "the words of the Word."

Jesus was the Teacher. Certainly He "taught with authority," and not as did the Scribes and Pharisees. Yet "He knew what was in man," and He did not trust Himself to the truly fickle crowds. He spoke in parables, mysteriously, mercifully - for pure hearts to understand.

Those who were seriously seeking the truth would "ponder," as did Mary His Mother, turning over and over in their hearts these mysterious sayings, until a bit of light should come. Those who were not really in earnest would hear and not understand and pass on to other, easier, more interesting things.

The same Jesus who said "The Father Himself loves you," would caution His followers not to cast their pearls before swine. Jesus was filled with the Holy Spirit of Wisdom. He spoke wisely, reticently, for those who really wanted to hear and to learn, to understand and to obey.

"The sower went out to sow His seed." Jesus was the Sower. The seeds were His words. Many of them would fall on dull, uncomprehending or shallow ears. Many of them would be choked by the thorns of care or smothered by the pleasures of the world. But some would find good ground, pure hearts, in which to grow and thrive and produce fruits of holiness.

"Some seeds fell on good ground." Some people would understand, and bear fruit, thirty, sixty or even a hundredfold, and this victory of the word would make all else worthwhile.

+

There would be many parables. This parable of the sower was only the first in a long series of wonderful teaching stories.

"The Kingdom of Heaven is like a man who sowed good seed in his field. But while everyone was asleep, his enemy came and sowed weeds among the wheat...."

"The Kingdom of Heaven is like a king who desired to settle accounts with his servants...."

"A certain man was going down from Jerusalem to Jericho, and he fell in with robbers...."

"The land of a certain rich man brought forth abundant crops, and he began to take thought within himself...."

"A certain man gave a great supper and invited many...."

"What man of you who has a hundred sheep, and losing one of them, does not leave the ninety-nine in the desert, and go after the one that is lost....?"

"A certain man had two sons, and the younger of them said to his father, 'Father, give me the share of the property that falls to me'...."

"There was a certain rich man who had a steward, and he was reported to him as squandering his possessions...."

"There was a certain rich man who used to clothe himself in purple and fine linen, and who feasted every day in splendid fashion...."

"Two men went up to the Temple to pray...."

"The Kingdom of Heaven is like a householder who went out early in the morning to hire laborers for his vineyard...."

"A certain nobleman went into a far country to obtain for himself a kingdom and then return. And he summoned ten of his servants and gave them ten gold pieces...."

"The Kingdom of Heaven is like a king who made a marriage feast for his son. And he sent out his servants to call in those invited...."

"It's like a man going abroad, who called his servants and delivered to them his goods. To one he gave five talents, to another two, and to another one...."

And there were more - seeds "cast into the earth," that would bear fruit in due time, as a farmer "goes to sleep and rises again, night and day," and the seed sprouts and grows "without his taking any thought of it." They were seeds of the Kingdom sown by the King, and they were beginning to do their quiet, unobtrusive work in the world into which He had come - till someday "of itself" the earth should bear the crop, "first the blade, then the ear, then the full grain in the ear," and "when the fruit is ripe," the Lord of the harvest should send His "angel with the sharp sickle," because now "the harvest is ready."

How many parables were there? We don't know. We only know that more than a dozen have survived, not counting the shorter ones. The parable is a literary form almost entirely peculiar to Jesus. He seems to have loved it. And indeed it is well suited to the expression of Mystery, to conveying religious truths, spiritual truths. The parables of Jesus convey extraordinary truths in the most ordinary ways. They speak of the sublime in terms of ordinary things that the common man, the poor man, can understand easily.

They speak of seeds, grains of wheat, farm fields, sheep and vineyards and working men, of kings and noblemen and rich men, of servants - industrious and lazy - of banquets and wedding celebrations, of the despised tax collector and the foolish youth.

They speak of the strict justice of God and of His incredibly beautiful mercy, "which is over all his works." They speak of His tender concern and His scandalous generosity. They bring home graphically such basic human values as common decency and consideration and compassion. They speak of reality - of enemies, of the enemy of the human race, the devil.

If the parable of the sower was the first, it seems to many of us that the utterly beautiful parable of the prodigal son, or as it has been called, of "the prodigal Father," is the greatest.

We all know the story. The boy asks for the share of the estate that is coming to him, and then heads off to enjoy it all recklessly. The inevitable follows - misery. He comes to himself and says "How many hired hands at my father's place have more than they can eat, and here I am starving. I will arise and go to my father and say to him, 'Father, I have sinned against Heaven and against you. I am no longer worthy to be called your son. Make me like one of your hired servants.'"

Meanwhile his father has been waiting out the days, and sees him coming, and runs "and falls on his neck" and kisses and embraces him. The boy has his little speech ready, "Father, I have sinned against Heaven and against you. I am no longer worthy to be called your son." But his father lets him get no further. Full of the joy of perfect love, he cries out, "Bring out the fattened calf, and let us celebrate. Get the best robe, and put it on him. For this my son was dead and has come to life again."

Surely we are all prodigal children to some extent. We are all sinners, and even the most innocent among us cannot fail to be moved, perhaps even to tears, by the exquisite beauty of the Father's goodness, kindness, gentleness, mercy, love. None of us need despair. Our God, our Father, is a God, a Father, of mercy and love, and not a Lord of cruel, strict and unrelenting justice.

If we choose sin, we will suffer, but it is not God's will that we be destroyed. He cannot stop the effects of the abuse of free will. But He lovingly waits, waits for us to "come to our senses," and realize that He Himself is only Love and Compassion, ever patiently awaiting our return.

The devil says to us, "He's mean. He's strict. If you go back to Him after all this sinning, He'll bawl you out, even if He does ultimately, grudgingly, take you back." But the Father Himself says, "No! I love you! Come to me, come to me in Jesus, all you who labor and are heavily weighted down under the burden of your own pride and self-sufficiency and foolishness. See that I am merciful and good, only longing to receive you back more tenderly than ever into my loving arms."

"The Lord is kind and merciful." If we sin, we bring suffering on ourselves, but God, Jesus, is our Savior precisely because we are sinners and need Him, not because we are all saints and can present Him with the perfect worship of our heroic virtue.

Heroic virtue is a gift that God often gives to repentant sinners, after they have learned the fundamental lesson of humility, the lesson that real love is always founded and rooted in profound humility. The real reason that we are not saints is that we are afraid of God. We cannot really believe that God can be good enough and big enough to surpass what we consider are either terrible sins or disgusting mediocrity and petty selfishness. But God is big, and God is good. And once we have humbly learned this basic lesson, His love, His grace, His goodness can begin to have its way with our hearts, can begin to transform us into heroes and heroines who "can do all things in Him" whose love gives us the strength and the power. A child has all the power of its strong Father. Having learned the fundamental lesson of total, childlike dependence, we are ready to set out along the way of perfect confidence and perfect love.

Actually, St. Benedict says we'll be there!

God is good. The Gospel is the Good News of His infinite love for us, manifested in the Christ who chose crucifixion to give us a picture of that love. But I dare say that this glorious parable of the prodigal son speaks the Father's love for us almost as eloquently as does the Crucifix itself.

+

"A certain man was going down from Jerusalem to Jericho...." The parable of the Good Samaritan might well be called the parable that our contemporary, depersonalized world needs most of all. We live in a largely heartless society. "Don't get involved."

And indeed, it's often dangerous. Things are not as simple as they were 2,000 years ago. Someone is mugged on a busy street corner in full daylight, and the passersby all timidly "mind their own business." We leave it for the police. We're not qualified.

And we pass on, like the priest and the Levite.

But this is not what Jesus Christ said to do. "Who in your opinion was neighbor to the man who fell among robbers?" We answer, "The man who took pity on him." And Jesus says to us, "Then go and do likewise."

It is not easy. It would be hard enough in a decent society. In our society it seems almost impossible.

We are driving along the highway. Somebody waves to us - obviously car trouble. But is it really? It could be fake. Could be a decoy, a trap. We keep on going.

We are timid. We have learned that we must take care of ourselves. If we don't, no one else will. We have learned the hard lesson of life, perhaps by honest experience.

But what have we really learned? That the Gospel is not really the truth?

We must read the Gospel. We must meditate on this parable. We must "stare" at its truth, until it breaks through the crust of all our strongly structured defenses.

We must pray for human hearts. We might even say that it would actually be better to die than to go on living so pitifully in a society where nobody can trust anybody else and everybody is afraid to show the least human concern for a brother or a sister in need, even sometimes for a close neighbor.

"Who is my neighbor?" Whoever needs my human

compassion and understanding and perhaps even physical assistance - he or she is my neighbor.

We cannot oversimplify. We cannot be simplistic. On the other hand, we must be true. The wonderful Holy Spirit's gift of wisdom, as we pray, will enable us to find a way to respond with genuine human compassion without subjecting ourselves foolishly to real danger. But the wisdom we need is, as St. Thomas Aquinas called it, "the wisdom of truth," not the "wisdom" of passing right on by.

+

"Two men went up to the Temple to pray." No one begins by thinking of himself or herself as a Pharisee. But until we have learned to pray, "O God, be merciful to me a sinner," we are all Pharisees. And it's not a lesson that comes easily.

We think we're not really bad people. We're pretty good Catholics, in comparison with a lot of others we know. "Humility does not consist in beating yourself down."

And it's just another way of saying, "I thank You, Lord, that I'm not like other people. I fast (maybe).... I tithe (to some extent)...." We're Pharisees, and it's humanly hopeless, because we think the real Pharisee is the other guy.

But it's not Divinely hopeless. "Nothing is impossible with God. With God all things are possible," even the things we don't realize, or even think, need to be done. The power of grace is infinite.

But "God resists the proud and gives grace to the humble." So then, how is His grace ever possibly going to be able to make its way to us?

Fortunately, humility is not the only virtue. We have a certain amount of ambition. We want to save ourselves from hell. We want to "go to Heaven," and in our better moments we even experience faint desires to be truly holy. Well then, "patience gains all things," even this beginning of real spiritual life, even this fundamental virtue of humility, which brings to our souls the sanctifying grace of God in all its fullness.

There is hope even for us Pharisees, if only we have the faith and patience to "keep on keepin' on" along the way of whatever prayer we can muster. For it seems that some of us blind Pharisees really do want the truth, though perhaps in a rather pathetic sort of way. In any case, God is very patient with all of us, and if we are patient with ourselves and persevere in prayer, someday we will surely learn to pray with conviction, "O God, be merciful to me a sinner," and perhaps our prayer will be all the purer for all the years of blindness that it took for us to arrive at the humility of the tax-collector.

"O God, be merciful to me a sinner!" In a slightly different form - "Lord Jesus Christ, have mercy on me a sinner!" - it was, as Pope John XXIII remarks, almost the only prayer of the great St. Francis of Assisi. It would seem, that in praying it, even frequently, we are in very good company.

"O God, be merciful to me a sinner!" Help me to overcome my blind pride and selfishness. Help me to see! Help me to overcome my sinfulness and to become holy. Transform me from a Pharisaical sinner into a truly great saint. This is Your will, that I be holy. Then, my God, make me holy. Make me the saint that You want me to be. In Jesus' name I pray, in the unity of the wonderful Holy Spirit. Amen.

+

"The Kingdom of Heaven is like a man who sowed good seed in his field. But while everyone was asleep, his enemy came and sowed weeds among the wheat...."

This parable of the weeds in the field is another one that we who endure the "reality" of life in the contemporary world need very much. The owner of the field told his servants not to pull up the weeds, or they would probably pull up the good wheat along with them, but to let both grow alongside each other until harvest time, and then when they harvested the wheat to discard and burn the weeds.

It makes a lot of sense. It is, of course, the only wise thing to do. But how much restraint it requires! All our natural instincts want a nice neat, pretty field. We want to get those awful weeds out of there, right now!

Yet if we look at the situation rationally, reflectively, they're not really doing any objective harm. The "enemy" is just trying to get us upset. The weeds are a pain to our egos, to our sense of what is appropriate and fitting. But that's all. They're a certain, perhaps we might say "esthetic," nuisance, but really no more.

We have to learn to live with them. Somebody has defined maturity as the ability to live with evil. The only problem is that this should not mean settling down to an acceptance of the evil and enjoying it - which is only too easy to do.

So there is a real Cross involved. We have to be in the world but not of it. Everybody is in the world today, even cloistered monks and nuns. The world reaches its tentacles even into contemplative monasteries. And it has to be, it seems, because the world is reality, and it's not all bad. The "*fuga mundi*" must not become a "flight from reality." The only answer for all of us is prayer, which alone will keep our religious idealism alive, a fire burning in our hearts. And we must not imagine that the holiness of any of the saints of past ages was ever unaccompanied by the stark reality of the subtle and perhaps nearly maddening Cross presented to us by what Scripture calls "the world."

In our day the True and Holy Cross often takes the form for all of us of these exasperating, frustrating, ugly old weeds that seem to be absolutely everywhere, seeming to grow more thickly than the wheat itself. Sometimes it seems hard even to find the wheat, the weeds seem to be thriving so vigorously.

But the wheat is there, and both faith and reason tell us that the only thing to be done, really the only thing possible, is to let them both grow together and wait patiently for harvest time.

The Biblical solution is "faith and patience." And once again we must remind ourselves that patience really does "gain all things," even final and ultimate victory. We will not see final victory in this world, except to the extent that "our faith" is victory. But the wonderful Holy Spirit has told us that this faith of ours really is victory, precisely over "the world of weeds."

+

"It's like a man going abroad, who called his servants and delivered to them his goods. To one he gave five talents, to another two, and to another one...."

A talent was a sum of money. We know the story - how the man with the five talents gained five more and the man with the two talents gained two more, and each was rewarded and congratulated by their master. The man who played it safe and hid his one talent away and returned it to his master without any profit is the one who in the end loses everything.

The question is, why - really - didn't he put it in the bank? Maybe he was one of those super-cautious people who don't trust banks. Maybe the whole meaning of this parable is to point out to us the wisdom of living in basic contact with reality.

Banks are ordinarily safe. Depositing money in a good bank and reaping a modest interest is not at all foolish.

We all have talents, and we have to put them to work. For the great Therese of Lisieux there seems to have been only one talent, the priceless talent of love. Yet Thomas Aquinas was perhaps no less great a saint, and for him there was the talent of intelligence.

But few of us can be purely spiritual like St. Therese or angelically intelligent like St. Thomas. We have talents that find their outlet in the ordinary workaday world. We do things. We produce things. We are businessmen or nurses or cabinet makers or school teachers. Our world is not a world of nothing but ideas and pure intentions. It is a world of jobs that have to get done.

Our vocation in life is to find out what we do best, and do it. Sometimes it may take a long time to find out what one's real talents are. For St. Benedict Joseph Labre, it took a lifetime, after travelling all over Europe from one religious shrine to another, to end up dying as a tramp on the streets of Rome. His whole vocation had been simply to seek God's will in a world that really cares little about it, asking continually as he moved along, "My God, what do You want me to do?"

Others discover their talents quickly and spend the rest of their lives becoming holy by plain old hard work.

Most of us are maybe somewhere in between. In our youth we fumble around at one "job" or another, and then after some years finally settle into the kind of work that we seem to be able to do best.

But here too there can be a real Way of the Cross, that consists both in seeking to learn what our real talents are, and then in seeking honestly to develop them by a life of hard, creative work. It is a Way of the Cross, but we are sincerely seeking, and we are confident deep down in our hearts that our labor "is not in vain in the Lord."

+

"The Kingdom of Heaven is like a king who desired to settle accounts with his servants. When he had begun the settlement one was brought to him who owed him ten thousand talents. As he had no means of paying, his master ordered him to be sold, with his wife and children and all that he had, and payment to be made."

We know the rest. "Have patience with me, and I will

pay you all!" In mercy his master remits the debt. Then the servant goes out and finds one of his fellow servants who owes him "a hundred denarii," maybe something like a hundred dollars in comparison with ten million. He throttles him: "Pay me what you owe me!" The man makes the identically same prayer, "Have patience with me, and I'll pay you everything!" But he refuses and puts him in jail.

His fellow servants are upset and tell the master, and the master excoriates his merciless servant, and then "hands him over to the torturers" until he pays everything.

Then Jesus concludes, "So also my Heavenly Father will do to you, if you do not each forgive your brothers from your hearts."

This is a tough one. On the surface it's perfectly reasonable. "Blessed are the merciful, for they shall obtain mercy." But in real life we cannot see that we owe God ten thousand times more than we think our brother owes us. And so we seek "justice," and end up "handed over to the torturers" until we finally do come to realize through much purifying suffering and prayer how infinitely merciful God has been to us.

This parable applies to everybody. Even St. Therese of Lisieux spoke of "staying out in the cold" and suffering patiently after a fault until one has done sufficient penance to right matters. Perhaps there really is no other way to thoroughly learn this sublime virtue of mercy than by enduring being "handed over to the torturers."

The "head torturer" is our conscience. We do wrong, and we suffer for it. We wait and pray for the pain to "go away." And the God of mercy, speaking to us through the truth of our conscience, little by little enlightens us - but sometimes oh! so painfully! - on the injustice, inhumanity and selfishness of our attitude. In the end we finally break down and give in simply for the sake of peace.

We manage to smile at our brother or sister. We manage a word of friendship. We are so angry! Because the "culprit" doesn't even consider it was a fault! Yet we were hurt, but not as badly, by infinities, as Jesus Christ got hurt on His Cross by our hard, unyielding, angry hearts. We look at Him nailed there in perfect meekness, and then we are enabled to manage a smile, or a word, and the blessed peace of God begins slowly returning to our poor, pitiful, struggling little human heart.

VI

He Has Done All Things Well

St. Matthew says that "Jesus was going about all the towns and villages, teaching in their synagogues, and preaching the Good news of the Kingdom, and curing every kind of disease and illness." He would look at the crowds and be "moved with compassion for them, because they were bewildered and dejected, like sheep without a shepherd."

So He was always healing, so much so that a little later in His career, after one such wonderful "sign," the people would exclaim with reverent and astonished awe, "He has done all things well. He has made both the deaf hear and the mute speak."

It was true. He had made the blind see and the lame walk. He had made countless sick people well and had even raised the dead to life. Indeed He had "done all things well."

But having read and heard the Gospels for two millennia, we are in danger of taking all these wonders for granted. There are even no small numbers of theologians today who largely discount miracles as "motives of credibility." They emphasize almost exclusively that faith is a mysterious gift that comes as a result of "religious experience," hardly from logical reasoning.

Yet this is not what Jesus Christ said. In fact, He said the very opposite. It is good to be impressed by the sheer power of His Divine Personality. But to many of us who are weaker and need them, He said that if that were not enough to make us believe, we should at least "believe the works that I do."

For all of these "works" are done well. To anyone with the least bit of solid logic in him or her, they point to a supernatural Mystery, even if one feels no particular emotional "experience" at all.

And the supreme miracle, of course, the supreme sign, the supreme "work," was the Resurrection of Jesus Himself from the dead. There may be periods of darkness or aridity in our lives of faith when logic has little power to move us or give us any kind of "experience." But when they pass, as they always will, it is abundantly good to be able to return confidently to the light of truth that we have reasoned to in faith, to have that faith bolstered and shored up by the wonderfully sound logic that moves from miracles to certainty, and that rests peacefully in the knowledge that "Jesus Christ is the Lord" who has truly "done all things well."

+

"He has made the deaf hear and the mute speak." St. Augustine said that God "shouted" and "broke through" his spiritual deafness. And this same Jesus, who by His grace finally "got through" to the mind and heart of the great Augustine, has made countless other splendid preachers of the Faith by giving them the power to speak it as zealous apostles.

If we persevere in prayer and keep reading the Gospels, Jesus will make us hear also, and even enable us to speak His truth to all. We are timid because our faith is weak. We cannot hear the Word of God, because our world is cluttered up with a thousand other noises. And so we have nothing to say about God or the things of God. For all practical purposes we are just about as pagan as all the world around us.

We need to meditate on the Gospel, "the Good News" of "this Jesus" who "does all things well." The more we contemplate Him, the more fascinating He becomes. Then fascination becomes surrender, and surrender and complete submission fullness of love.

We have a little tiny bit of faith or we wouldn't even be concerning ourselves about Him. We pray for faith, from time to time, with more or less energy, perhaps as problems arise.

But we need to become systematic. We need to set apart every day a bit of time, more or less - preferably more, as possible - to sit and be still and read a page or two of this incomparable little book. Familiarity with the pages of the Gospels will lead to a certain quiet enjoyment in going over and over them, and this enjoyable "taste" for the Word of God at its best will lead to stronger, more living faith and a bolder confidence in Christ.

We may feel that it's all pretty near hopeless. The Gospels may even seem boring to us. And it's true that we do need to supplement them with the rest of the New Testament and the Psalms and the whole Bible and other spiritual reading. But a lot is merely surface repugnance. There is power in these pages. We must keep coming back to those wonderful words of "the greatest saint of modern times," Therese of Lisieux, and realize that our "feeble efforts" are all God needs to make us truly and sublimely holy.

Take up the Gospels. Read a paragraph, or a page. If you seem to get nothing out of it, try it again the next day. It will not take many days of searching before you find something, something precious, meant just for you, a "pearl of great price" hidden in these fields of the Scriptures, a treasure that will stay with you permanently. It may be a sentence, it may be a phrase, it may be a single word. But it will be a special and unique gift of Our Lord Jesus Christ to your own individual and unrepeatable heart. It may even be this very line - "He has done all things well."

+

Jesus was a miracle of joy for the poor everywhere He went. Especially in His tangles with the Pharisees, yet certainly not only in these, the common people rejoiced beyond measure at all the things that were so "gloriously" done by Him. Indeed, it was a glorious thing for Truth to publicly and openly flout hypocrisy, for Freedom to boldly triumph over the most stifling adherence to the letter of a dying law, for Goodness and Love and Mercy to be completely victorious everywhere over the common narrowminded pettiness that ordinarily rules this dark world.

It was joy and it was glory, this life of Jesus Christ in our midst. It was to last, in all the splendor of its public phase, perhaps a little over two full years. That was not really too very long, nor was it all pure triumph. There was persecution, continual petty nagging by the religious authorities, which toward the end began breaking out into physical attempts on His life. To us looking back from the vantage point of our century much of it seems simply ridiculous. Yet it was steadily increasing in seriousness, and would in the end mean for Jesus condemnation to death as a criminal.

It was absurd. It was surrealism. It was "religion" carried beyond the world, the realm, of meaning. It was the insane "corruption of the best." Jewish monotheism, the gift of God to the whole world, was being converted into the instrument of Deicide.

It was more than paradoxical. It was most strange. It was weird. Really, it was diabolical. We know this by faith, and it is the only satisfactory answer.

But do we dare blame a people of another age and race, of a far corner of the world, of a foreign culture, "different" than we are? All sin is diabolical. When I shut my eyes in little things and fail to do the truth, it is an added ounce of weight to the terrible Cross of Jesus Christ. When I am dishonest or unfaithful, when I choose expedience over the right, I concur with Caiaphas in his judgment that Jesus should die.

I don't want to do wrong. I don't want to choose evil. But I want to "survive." I want to be "happy."

I want "love and happiness." But when love and fidelity mean considerable suffering, what do I choose?

The Holy Spirit says, "Choose life!" Take up the Gospel of Jesus Christ, "the Gospel of Life." The Life of Christ is our own by sanctifying grace. We do not feel it. Yet it is there for us to contemplate, to see in the pages of the Gospels. If we persevere in reading, we are enabled to see, to realize, that "He has done all things well."

He has the answers, the answers that we all need. He has all the answers, as the God-Man. He has them for us one by one, as we need them. He has, He is, the Truth Personified, Truth that will free us - once and for all, if we will have it so - from slavery to passion, human respect and our own sheer, lazy egotism.

+

We may ask how the Pharisees could have made such a big thing out of a phenomenon of which we ourselves might have remarked, "It's only religion." There was no question of murder or robbery or any real crime, as Pilate was quick to see.

Yet perhaps this is simply a sign of the kind of society in which we live today. We think of religion as a bland, mild, innocuous kind of thing. Perhaps the most terrible thing about our contemporary society is the fact that for some decades now no one really gets excited about religion any more. Instead it seems largely ignored as a pretty nearly dead thing.

In a truly religious society, it is a thing of deep passion and profound conviction. Whatever we may say about the Pharisees, this much is certainly true - that they were very serious about religion.

Pilate they probably could have assassinated if they had wanted to badly enough. But Pilate was not really a threat to them. He left them more or less alone. But Jesus did not.

In reality Jesus Christ does not leave anybody alone. He says to all of us things like "Be perfect," "Be holy," "Be merciful."

There is no room for another God in our lives besides Him. He claims everything.

But He likewise gives us the gift of giving Him everything He asks for.

He gives us the Gift of Love. This seems to be the one gift, with its companion humility, that the Pharisees were without. They certainly had the gift of religion. And they had a very real faith, at least of some kind. But their hearts were not right. It is with the heart that one sees, and they could not see.

They thought they could see, and Jesus said that was precisely what made them blind. Their real blindness lay in not realizing that they were blind.

They asked, "Are we blind?" And Jesus answered that the Light was only going to be in the world a little while longer. They should walk while they had the Light.

We ourselves are not so terribly different. The Light is actually extremely bright. It seems that even the great Thomas Aquinas, as Scripture itself advises, "chose wisdom," the "wisdom of truth," rather than the pure Light as such. But we ourselves often choose the "wisdom" of expedience.

This "wisdom of truth" is itself a very demanding thing. But maybe for us less magnificent souls what has been called "the wisdom of patience" will be in the end a no less real and effective wisdom. If we cannot take "the way of truth" straight, in all its terrible austerity, maybe we can travel, with no less spiritual success, the path of humility, which is really the wonderful path of love, that love which "is patient," with that patience which "gains all things."

Certainly there are times when the path of humility and love seems every bit as terrible as any "way of truth" ever could be. Surely it is itself somehow a genuine way of truth. We may at times even be able to say with the wondrous Little Flower that we did not know it was "possible to suffer so much." And we keep our sanity only because of Him "who does all things well," and heals all who come to Him, not only the deaf and mute, but the lame, and most especially, the blind as well.

Was it not St. Clement of Alexandria who said that "Humility, like darkness, reveals the Heavenly Light"?

+

Jesus "cured every kind of disease and illness." But He can't cure mine, we think - mine is different. Or even if He can, He might not want to. Mine is one of those abnormal modern maladies. What can He do about depression? We are no longer living in the age of miracles. The only thing to do is put up with the doctors and get along as best you can.

On the other hand, why not try prayer? Prayer itself

can be a completely calming miracle. In prayer one can often find a real reason to go on "living and hoping." By prayer one taps Divine Power. Surely Jesus Christ means something when He says, "No one who comes to me will I reject." This is a promise that every prayer is heard and answered.

In answering our prayers God keeps first things first. Our salvation and sanctification come before our financial success or even our health. But all things come in their proper time and order to him or her who prays, and keeps on praying.

"Well, I prayed, and He didn't heal me. I feel just as miserable as ever." And what did you pray for? "Healing!" But maybe you don't even know what healing is. You prayed for happiness, and you're still suffering. But maybe it would be better to pray for the grace to suffer well, the grace to grow through suffering, the grace to be victorious in faith rather than simply relieved of a bothersome burden.

"No one who comes to me will I reject." That's our faith. It has to be that the way of prayer, even as a way of suffering, is a better way than the world's way of smooth and urbane despair. If we pray we'll be healed, on the deepest level, the level of unbelief. Faith itself is the only real, and actually the ultimate, victory in this world. Faith brings true peace and true happiness, even if it does not immediately bring the bliss of Heaven.

We need to learn, even in our suffering, to make acts of faith in the truth that "He has done all things well." If He allows us to suffer, it is not because He wants us to suffer, but because we must grow. Scripture says, He says, “In crushing misfortune, be patient.” But He also tells us through His saints, when we are in difficult straits, to “try everything!” - and He will come to meet us in this prayer of sincere effort.

Jesus does not work miracles except for those who do what they can to meet Him “half way” in faith. On the other hand, this prayer of faith, when it is truly fervent, works tremendous miracles, infallibly. Faith itself is perhaps the greatest miracle of all. More often than not, Jesus said it was their faith itself that healed the people who came to Him. All He did was accept that faith lovingly.

But even if we are healed, the way of faith remains a difficult Way of the Cross. We live by faith and not by sight. We must work hard all our lives in this world at this way of faith. We must keep our faith alive and growing stronger and stronger. We must persevere in prayer, and this very prayer of faith will make us and keep us whole with that wholeness which is identical with holiness itself.

+

Jesus Christ cures everybody who comes to Him with the sincere desire to be cured, to be healed truly and on the deepest level, the level of the spirit at least. He does not always eliminate suffering. In fact, where He finds a noble soul, worthy of accompanying Him in the apostolate, He may allow the suffering to increase. But even if He does, He gives increased joy and strength and victory in a faith that He makes stronger even out of all proportion.

Faith is a very great good. Love in faith can advance to a far greater perfection than it would ever be able to without this preeminently "Gospel" virtue, because faith gives love its true object, Jesus Christ, the God-Man.

"This is the victory....our faith," faith that "does not need a three-ring circus" all the time, faith that can look out on the plain old world of everyday existence and see, as God saw in the beginning, that it is still "very good."

The rain is good, and the sunshine is good, and which is better only God really knows. Absolutely speaking, light is better than darkness - and "there will be no night" in Heaven, only Eternal Sunshine. Yet now in this unfinished world of time, the precious, cooling, refreshing, lifegiving rain, on the dark grey days, can be a wonderfully blessed thing, for those who need a little "quiet time," and have learned how to see that it too is "very good."

We live in Mystery. It is partly because God Himself is simply infinitely holy beyond all our intellectual capacities, and partly too because the darkness of sin has immensely complicated the world and God must work the very darkness into His all-encompassing plan. But He will use - and even now is using - this very darkness to make an even more beautiful thing than the world would have been without sin.

"O Happy Fault!" which has brought us a grace not only more abundant than the original sin, or all sin put together, but even greater, from the point of view of our spiritual dignity, than the grace that the first man had in the beginning. It may be argued that all grace is necessarily the same. Yet the Church teaches in her Liturgy that the grace of our dignity in Christ is somehow, mysteriously, greater than what we had in the beginning.

Jesus Christ has not merely repaired sin. He has super-repaired it. He has furthered evolution. He has brought progress. If there were for us today no real progress over Adam's state, there would actually be no real hope. But in Christ we are somehow better off than Adam was. We have lost the preternatural gifts, but we have gained in the purely supernatural order of grace, faith and love a somehow infinitely greater dignity in our vocation to suffer and triumph with the Crucified and Risen Jesus.

There is for us who know and love Christ Jesus a new "gift of integrity," not preternatural, but supernatural, moral and "theological," far greater in value, which Jesus Christ gives to all who come to Him in the prayer of sincere and living faith.

+

We are all in need of healing, and he who did all things well during His life on earth will heal us all if only we come to Him with faith and confidence and ask to be healed.

Lord, make us whole! In this utterly sick society in which we live, there is not a single one of us, anywhere, who cannot make this prayer his or her own in truth and reality.

We are all sick, and those who don't realize it are the worst off of all. We need the healing earth, the healing woods and streams and hills and lakes and mountains - but most of all we need the healing Jesus in His Most Blessed Sacrament and Sacrifice of the Eucharist and in His Holy Gospel.

Jesus Christ, crucified and now risen, continues to do all things well, even when He allows us to suffer as part of the process of our healing. Indeed, in a soft and indulgent society it is good to suffer. The discipline of suffering is the only means we have in this awful world of attaining to true wholeness. It can be extremely painful, but it leads always to the victory of peace.

"Shalom!" It means the fullness of peace. It means wholeness. And it is the special gift of Jesus Christ to all of us who come to Him. "I leave you peace.... my peace," not the peace that the world gives, which merely covers over profound problems. The peace of Jesus is the solution to all problems, because it consists in order. It is the stillness, the fullness of order.

How good it is to experience the healing, the wholeness that Christ gives - to be able to look out at the beauty of an ordinary tree in the summertime and find joy in its green leaves and branches gently stirring in the breeze. The prayer of quiet can be the gift of Jesus on a mild day in June.

"He has done all things well." The crowds could see it. It was obvious, perfectly evident. He was simple, and they were simple. He was giving gifts in all simplicity, and they who knew they needed Him were accepting them with all simplicity and gratitude.

It was wonderful to follow and to contemplate this gift-giving Jesus, this Holy Healer who was Kindness

Personified, walking through towns and villages, bringing happiness, wholeness everywhere He went.

If we too follow Him in faith, he will heal us, "whole" us, by means of that very faith, and perhaps all unbeknownst to ourselves, imperceptibly, as we "keep on keepin' on" down the trails of life and time, in the footsteps of Him who has gone before us. We may not even formulate an explicit request. We may only have the energy, like the man who had been ill for 38 years, to state our problem, or perhaps only the energy to pray the prayer of simply going on, or even less, of just waiting - in hope. But there are many kinds and forms of prayer, and Jesus Christ is sensitive to them all. At the bare minimum, if only we "wait for the Lord," healing and wholing will come in due time from Him who is sure to pass our way sooner or later.

+

Christ was patient, not only with the Pharisees and the crowds, but even with the denseness of His close disciples. He is likewise patient with us, who perhaps rank among the very densest of His followers. The only problem lies with us. We too must be patient, patient with ourselves, and with the workings of God's providence. We want to be healed, to be whole, to be perfectly healthy - in every way - now!

Well, it takes time. Like the man who received his sight in stages - "I see people, but they look like trees walking around" - we too must have the patience to let God heal us in His own way and time. He will do it, surely, certainly, but not always at once, and not always in the way we imagine He should or hope He will. He does it in His own way and time, more thoroughly than we could ever conceive. He heals us from the spirit "down" or "outward" or however you want to say it. He heals the whole person, but beginning with the spirit, the mind and will and heart.

There are many things we need to be healed of, spiritual problems perhaps even more than the physical ones so prominent in the pages of the Gospels. We need to be healed of spiritual blindness, spiritual deafness. We need to have many devils cast out - demons of pride and lust, insecurity and fear, anger and anxiety. We may be spiritually lame or paralyzed, hardly able to take a step forward down the path of life. Or we may even need to be brought back to the life of grace and faith, love and prayer.

One thing is sure - we all need healing, and Jesus Christ is the world's foremost Healer, and He always will be. In an age when the whole medical profession is becoming more and more corrupt, this wonderful healing power of Jesus Christ is coming more and more to the fore. People are becoming both disgusted and desperate, even desperate enough to turn to religion, even to prayer.

It will, of course, work. We have tried everything else. Now let us try faith in Jesus Christ. For us who thought we had lost all hope, there is joy in the very phrase. "Faith in Jesus Christ" - St. Thomas Aquinas says it is our first means of approach to God.

We make our desperate act of faith. We kneel down - or perhaps throw ourselves down full length, prostrate on the ground - and we pray as we have never prayed before. We pray for deliverance from the demon - it may very well be "Legion" - of meaninglessness or hopelessness or depression or near despair. We pray for peace, for wholeness, for fullness of being and life. We pray for survival, and even for salvation.

We pray - and the God who hears and answers every prayer strengthens our heart and mind and will to become calm and quiet. He says simply, "I am with you." And we know that that is all we need, and we find ourselves suddenly on the road to victory.

+

When Jesus Christ heals people, they stay healed - because He doesn't do it except for the good of the soul, that is, of the whole being. This is the explanation for much suffering in our lives. Our motives are not pure. We want happiness in order to squander it, and we don't even realize this. If our first priority is the salvation and sanctification of our souls, in reality and not just in theory, we will get everything else we ask for. If we truly "seek first the Kingdom of God and His justice, all these other things" will be given us besides.

This means purification, painful purification - sometimes years or even decades of purification. How wise was St. Augustine: "Lord, purify me in this world!" The road to true and lasting happiness is usually a long and painful Way of the Cross. We have free will, and we have to master it. We have to direct it toward the real good in a world of a million counterfeits. We have to overcome our pride, our passions, our egotism, a thousand disorders of body and soul. This is the work of a lifetime.

The healing gift that Jesus Christ gives us is first of all the simple presence of His Holy Spirit in our hearts, to teach us the faith and the love that will assure final victory. Indeed, the real victory is simply to have learned to live by faith.

We want to be healed in order to be happy. But we don't know what happiness is. Real happiness consists in giving, until we are one with Jesus Christ who gave everything on the Cross of suffering. Real happiness consists in the gift of mystical union with God and all our brothers and sisters "in the Spirit."

Wholeness is based on this mystical union. And the road to it is long and hard. But Christ gives us everything we need for the journey, including Himself to be our strengthening and sustaining Nourishment along the way in the Eucharist.

Wholeness is based on oneness with God and with His creation. It is based on the wonderful "unity of the Holy Spirit."

Holiness is wholeness, and wholeness consists in complete moral, intellectual and spiritual "integrity." It is identical with "the justice that is of faith," with the grace of that strong, living faith which is itself our total victory.

There are many routes to this spiritual victory, but they are all ways of complete and total dependence on Christ, on His grace, His Holy Spirit, His Mother Mary, His saving and sanctifying will, His presence in the Eucharist and in the whole Church, the family of God.

We all want to be healed. We all want to live fully, to be vibrant with health and vitality. But we usually don't really know what it means. We want to have what we have seen in other people, but if those others were anything less than saints, and sometimes even if they were saints, it can be misleading, for holiness and wholeness consist in becoming what we personally are called to be, which may mean something worlds apart even from our favorite saint.

Each of us is unique. I am called to achieve holiness and wholeness in a completely different way from St. Francis of Assisi or St. Therese of Lisieux. Perhaps there are many saints who can be models for me up to a point. But sooner or later, if I am to become the saint that God wants me to be, I have to give up all the images and ideas and pre-conceived notions that I have acquired from them, and launch out onto the way of faith that will make me perfectly dependent on Jesus alone, the only Bridegroom of my soul.

I must learn, at the proper point in time, in the course of my spiritual development, to "let go" of many good things that my favorite saint said or did, in order to move onward to what God is calling Me to be and do. I may have depended on Saint So-and-so for decades, but there will come a time, if I am to become a saint myself, that I must learn in faith to move beyond my hero or heroine to the God of love and holiness Himself.

All this is very painful. Being healed of spiritual diseases can be very painful. Even advancing to greater spiritual health and wholeness can be very painful. "In order to become a saint it is necessary to suffer very much," said the Little Flower. This is profoundly true. And yet we must move even beyond our theory of suffering to absolute docility to the Holy Spirit, in joy and pain both.

Masochism is not holy. Suffering itself is not as holy as the Holy Spirit is. It may be said that Jesus "became Suffering" for us as He hung crucified on Calvary. Yet Jesus became primarily obedient.

He heals us, makes us whole, primarily by bringing us His wonderful Holy Spirit to make us holy. It is possible to misunderstand the saints and in spite of ourselves to make a cult of suffering that does no good at all. We must not only suffer very much to become holy, but we must also suffer according to God's will, not according to our own - and this can mean an infinitely bewildering purification.

"A sad saint is a sorry saint." A saint without joy is no saint at all. The saints speak truly of suffering while on a deeper level they are full of spirit - the Holy Spirit of Jesus Christ. Suffering that depresses us and deprives us of this spirit, though like all suffering it must be borne patiently, is nevertheless from the devil and not from God.

We must pray much to the wonderful Holy Spirit, not precisely to load us with sufferings, but to make us holy as He is holy. We must pray to Jesus Christ our Lord to heal us and whole us, and this may often very well mean praying simply for peace.

"Peace is love," said St. John of the Cross. Peace is healing. "Shalom!" It is the peculiar gift of "this Jesus."

Unless You Eat the Flesh of the Son of Man

To take up the Gospel story more or less where we left off, it seems that at about this point Jesus decided to call together the Twelve and give them power over the devils and power to heal, and then to send them out two by two to preach the Kingdom of God and "to cure every kind of disease and illness."

It seems also that while they were out on this mission, with Jesus Himself preaching and teaching independently, that Herod put John the Baptizer to death. So when the Twelve returned to Jesus "and reported to Him all that they had done and taught," He said to them - partly because they were all fatigued and partly to spiritually assimilate the passing of John - "Come aside into a deserted spot and rest awhile." For there were many people "coming and going," so that they hardly had leisure even to eat.

They got into their boat and headed off across the lake.

But the people, actually crowds, saw where the boat was headed, "and hurried to the place on foot from all the towns, and got there ahead of them."

They landed, and Jesus "went up the mountain," and sat down there "with His disciples." St. John remarks that "the Passover, the Feast of the Jews, was near."

The Gospel goes on, "When, therefore, Jesus had lifted up His eyes" - we may perhaps add "weary eyes" - "and seen that a very great crowd had come to Him, He had compassion on them, because they were like sheep without a shepherd. And He began to teach them many things, and spoke to them of the Kingdom of God, and those in need of cure He healed."

"Now when the day was far spent," His disciples came to Him and said, "This is a deserted spot, and the hour is already late." The crowds needed to be dismissed so that they could go get themselves something to eat. "But Jesus said to them, 'They don't need to go away. You yourselves give them some food.'"

They said to Him, "Are we to go and buy two hundred denarii worth of bread and give them something to eat?"

Then Jesus said to Philip, "Where are we going to buy bread for these people to eat?" St. John remarks that "He said this to try them, for He Himself knew what He was going to do."

Philip answered Him, "Two hundred denarii worth of bread would not be enough for them," even for each one to receive just a little.

Then Jesus said to them all, "How many loaves have you? Go and see."

When they had found out, Andrew said to Him, "There is a young boy here who has five barley loaves and two fishes, but what are these among so many?"

Jesus said, "Bring them here to me."

Then "He ordered them to make all the people recline in groups on the green grass. And they reclined in groups of hundreds and fifties. And He took the five loaves and the two fishes and looking up to Heaven, blessed and broke the loaves and gave them to His disciples to set before the people."

"And all ate and were satisfied."

When they had all eaten, Jesus said to the disciples, "Gather the fragments that are left over, so that they don't go to waste." They gathered them up and filled twelve baskets with the fragments of the five barley loaves left over. "Now the number of those who had eaten was five thousand men, not counting women and children."

St. John says that when the people had seen the "sign" Jesus had worked, they said, "This really is the Prophet who is to come into the world."

Jesus saw their enthusiasm, that they would try to "take Him by force and make Him King." So "He made His disciples get into the boat and cross the sea ahead of Him," while He Himself dismissed the crowd. "And when He had dismissed them, He went away to the mountain to pray."

Meanwhile it had become dark. The Apostles were out in their boat, and "the sea was rising, because a strong wind was blowing." The boat was being tossed about on the waves, "for the wind was against them."

Then, "seeing them straining at the oars....about the fourth watch of the night," Jesus came to them, "walking on the sea." When they saw Him, they cried out, "It's a ghost!" Jesus said to them, "Courage! It is I! Don't be afraid!"

Peter said, "Lord, if it's You, tell me to come to You over the water." Jesus said, "Come." Peter got out of the boat and started walking on the water toward Jesus, but seeing the strong wind, grew afraid. "And as he began to sink he cried out, 'Lord, save me!'" Jesus put out His hand and took hold of him and said to him, "0 you of little faith, why did you doubt?"

They got into the boat, and the wind fell. The Apostles worshipped Jesus, "You really are the Son of God!" They were astonished - "and immediately the boat was at the land toward which they were going."

"The next day, the crowd which had remained on the other side of the sea observed that there had been only one boat there, and that Jesus had not gone into the boat with His disciples, but that they had departed alone." Then other boats from Tiberias came along, and the crowd used them to come to Capernaum, "seeking Jesus."

When they found Him, they said to Him, "Rabbi, when did You come here?"

Jesus said to them, "I tell you truly, you seek me, not because you have seen signs, but because you have eaten of the loaves and have been filled. Do not work for the food that perishes, but for that which endures to eternal life, which the Son of Man will give you."

They said to Him, "What are we to do to do the works that God wants?" Jesus said to them, "This is the work of God, for you to believe in Him whom He has sent." They said to Him, "What sign do you do, then, for us to see and believe You? What work do You perform? Our fathers had the manna in the desert, as it is written, 'He gave them bread from Heaven to eat.'"

Jesus said, "I tell you truly, it was not Moses who gave you the Bread from Heaven. It is my Father who gives you the real Bread from Heaven. The Bread of God is that which comes down from Heaven and gives life to the world."

They said to Him, "Lord, give us this bread always!" Jesus said to them, "I am the Bread of Life. Whoever comes to me will not hunger, and whoever believes in me shall never thirst. But I have told you that you have seen me, and you do not believe."

They began murmuring about this saying of His, "I am the Bread that has come down from Heaven." They kept saying to one another, "Isn't this Jesus, the Son of Joseph, whose father and mother we know? How can He say, 'I have come down from Heaven'?"

Jesus went on, "I am the Bread of Life. Your fathers ate the manna in the desert, and died. This is the Bread that comes down from Heaven, so that if anyone eats of it he will not die. I am the Living Bread that has come down from Heaven. If anyone eat of this Bread, he shall live forever. The Bread that I will give is my flesh for the life of the world."

They began arguing with one another, "How can this man give us His flesh to eat?"

Then Jesus said to them, "I tell you truly, unless you eat the flesh of the Son of Man and drink His blood, you shall not have life in you. Whoever eats my flesh and drinks my blood has eternal life, and I will raise him up on the last day. For my flesh is real food, and my blood is real drink. Whoever eats my flesh and drinks my blood lives in me and I in him."

"As the Living Father has sent me, and as I live because of the Father, so whoever eats me shall also live because of me. This is the Bread that has come down from

Heaven, but not as your fathers ate the manna and died. Whoever eats this Bread will live forever."

When they heard this talk about eating His flesh, many of them said, "This is a hard saying! Who can take it?"

Jesus, knowing that they were murmuring among themselves, said to them, "Does this scandalize you? What then if you should see the Son of Man ascending to where He was before? It's the spirit that gives life. The flesh is useless."

He went on, "The words that I have spoken to you are spirit and life. But there are some among you who do not believe." He said, "This is why I have told you, 'No one can come to me unless he is enabled to do so by my Father.'"

And at this point St. John says, "From this time many of His disciples turned back and no longer went about with Him."

So Jesus said to the Twelve, "Do you want to go away too?" Peter answered, "Lord, to whom shall we go? You have the words of eternal life, and we have come to believe and to know that You are the Christ, the Son of God."

Jesus said to them, "Haven't I chosen all Twelve of you? Yet one of you is a devil." St. John says, "He was speaking of Judas Iscariot....for he it was, though one of the Twelve, who was to betray Him."

+

The Eucharist! "Thanks be to God for His unspeakable Gift!" And yet what a mercy it is for us to live now when we do. If we had heard those words from the lips of Jesus, we too might have walked away. In His infinite mercy Jesus Christ has prepared us for this exquisitely beautiful Gift by leading us up to it gently. We have been instructed in the meaning of sacraments as signs, in the meaning of the Eucharistic signs of bread and wine, transformed by the wonder of "transubstantiation" into Christ's own Body and Blood, His very Self, to be our pleasant spiritual Nourishment.

How gently He has led us, to a peaceful understanding of the wonderful Eucharistic Mystery. Yet even today, how many there are for whom these are "hard words," to be accepted symbolically - and only symbolically. Yet as Catholics we believe in the "true, real and substantial" presence of Jesus Christ, "Body and Blood, Soul and Divinity," in this greatest of the sacraments, "under the appearances of bread and wine."

We eat the Flesh of Jesus Christ, and we drink His Precious Blood, and there is peace, prayer, grace. He has arranged, ordered all things beautifully, sweetly, fittingly. We receive Him in Holy Communion as our spiritual Food, spiritual Nourishment for the journey of life through this world.

We believe in Him, and He works this Miracle of Joy for us all. Yet we must maintain the Doctrine, profess the Truth, or our own grace and gift of faith will weaken and fail.

We come to Him in this Sacrament. "No one who comes to me will I reject." We come humbly, fearfully, confidently, believing, trusting - and with our Holy Communion He brings us peace and strength.

Jesus knew who were the ones who didn't believe, and

who was the one who would betray Him. It was the Eucharist, the Doctrine of the Eucharist, that was the real stumbling block, and the beginning of Judas' turning away.

Jesus had reached the high point of His public career. This crowd of five thousand men was perhaps the largest. The next time there will be four thousand. His popularity will continue to diminish, it seems, until on Good Friday everyone abandons Him - except His Mother Mary, the Apostle John, Mary Magdalen, and a few other women.

Yes, we have, it seems, reached the climax of Jesus' triumphant expansion throughout the whole land. From now on there will be a steady waning. The Eucharist, as it has been called, is the Sacrament of Truth. And with its announcement in Jesus' life we have reached the moment of truth.

The way of truth, the word of truth, the wisdom of truth - always truth, truth, truth! It is the gift of Jesus. It is the Truth, the wonderful, liberating Truth, that must either be accepted completely and absolutely, humbly and lovingly, or rejected, contradicted, fought. There is no middle course. Even apparent indifference is really a proud contempt for it, or a subtly disguised angry antagonism, or a hatred too great for visible manifestation.

Yet "poor sinners" simply lack the power to believe. Living faith is a grace and a gift, and we who are blessed with it, we who have been enabled by God to believe, are bound to pray and suffer and work to bring this Eucharistic faith to all those who, if they had the gift, might very well be far more fervent and devoted than we are who perhaps take it lazily for granted, at least to some extent.

The Eucharist! The very word means "Thanksgiving,"

"Gratitude." And surely it is the perfect word. For so great a Gift what else can we do but be infinitely, profoundly, utterly grateful. "I am with you all days, even to the consummation of the world," with you in my Holy Spirit in the community of faith, hope and love, spiritually, but with you in this Sacrament in a way that you can see and feel and taste. I am with you, warmly, lovingly, faithfully, permanently, substantially, really, truly.

O Lord Jesus Christ, thank You for this Gift, for this Gift of Yourself! Thank You for Your universal availability. Thank You for Your Real Presence in all the tabernacles of the world. Thank You for the Eucharistic Sacrament and Sacrifice. Thank You, my God! Have mercy on us all! Increase our faith in You here in Your Sacramental Presence. Never let us walk away. Protect us all, always, by the infinite "power of this Sacrament." Amen.

+

The wonderful workings of God's Providence are all of a piece. Here is a crowd of five thousand men, not counting women and children, gathered together around Jesus and the Twelve, out in a deserted spot, out in the middle of nowhere. It's evening, and they're all getting hungry. They have got themselves into this fix for love of Him.

Jesus knows the situation. He has been aware of it as it has been developing. He knows what He is going to do. He has foreseen the whole development of these events from all Eternity. Everything is working itself into His plan, His Father's plan, for the salvation "of the whole human race."

The people are hungry. They need supper. But it is

apparently a problem. Jesus says to Philip, "Where are we going to get bread for all these people? What are we going to do, Philip?" He is almost playful. He is almost teasing him. He is drawing him on to make an act of faith. As St. John says, He Himself knows what He is going to do.

The people need a good supper. Jesus will provide them with a supper that will be a continuation of the Old Testament miracle of the manna, and a foreshadowing of the Eucharistic miracle that He will work at the Last Supper on Holy Thursday Evening.

The people are hungry. Jesus will feed them. Mankind is hungry. Jesus, the God-Man, will feed us all. He will use this scene, this situation, this event, to announce what He plans to do in the future, what He came into the world to do - to bring to all of us in Sacramental form the Reality of His Sacrificial Offering of Himself as the Lamb that was slain to be our spiritual Food, the Bread of our Eternal Life and the Divine Wine that will bring us everlasting joy.

The people will not understand the meaning of "the sign." Not even the Apostles will understand, not even Peter. Many who do not understand will go away and follow Jesus no longer, because they are incapable of believing, of going beyond understanding. Some, who do not understand any more than the others, will remain with Jesus because they have come "to believe and to know" that He is the Christ, the Son of the Living God.

"What sign do You work? Our fathers had the manna in the desert." He had just worked a sign almost identical with the manna, but for the blind there is no seeing. They ate the bread, but Jesus said they did not see the sign. They sought Him as one who would Satisfy only the hunger of their bodies. They saw the bread, but they did not see the sign. They did not see the bread for the sign that it really was.

Therefore they would not be able to understand when Jesus continued in the language of signs. He spoke of His flesh as Bread. It was unacceptable. It remains unacceptable today to very many. Many are still unable to see the sign. People see the bread. They do not see the Sign. They do not see by faith the Body of Christ. In His mercy God has given us who believe the eyes to see what cannot be seen. He has given us the eyes of faith.

It looks like bread. It tastes like bread. And it is the Body of Christ.

It looks like wine. It tastes like wine. And it is His Precious Blood.

It is the Food of the Strong. It is Divine Bread, Divine Wine. It is Someone. It is God Himself, coming to us to unite us to Himself in the spiritual union of perfect love. It is the "*Signun Unitatis*," the "*Vinculum Caritatis*" - the Sign of Unity, the Bond of Love.

It is the Whole of Reality. It is Jesus, the God-Man, assimilating us to Himself, transforming us into Himself in a manner precisely the opposite of that in which we transform ordinary food into ourselves.

It is our assimilation to the Sacrifice of Christ, to His Crucifixion and Resurrection. It is our incorporation ever more fully and deeply into His Mystical Body, the Whole Christ, the Church.

It is the Memorial of His suffering and death, in which the mind is filled with grace and there is given us a powerful pledge of future glory.

It is the Mystery of Faith. It is the "*Sacramentum*

Pietatis" - the Sacrament or Mystery of Fidelity, of "Piety," of Loyalty, of Loving Kindness, Mercy, Compassion.

It is the Sacrament of All Things, the greatest of all the sacraments, the Sacrament of Sacraments, the Effective Sign toward which all other signs are ordered.

It makes present to the whole world, to every part of the world in every age, the Sacrifice that was offered on the Mountain called Calvary when the hour of Jesus Christ had come.

It is Sacrament and Sacrifice, Sacramental Sacrifice. The separate consecration of the bread and wine place the Body and Blood of Jesus on the altar separately, in an immolated state, mystically re-presenting, in an "unbloody" manner, the loss of His Precious Blood from His Holy Body at the hour of His crucifixion.

The slain and risen Jesus enters into our very being, in order that we may enter into Him. He is the Bridegroom, and we are the Bride. Eucharistic union is the most intimate of all unions, impossible even to conceive of except for a Divine Lover. The Eucharist, far more than Matrimony, is the Sacrament of Love. It is indeed a transcendent Matrimony, a mystical Marriage, between God and the soul, between Christ and the Church.

It is the Sign of Unity and the Bond of Charity - it makes the unity of the people of God and keeps the community together in faith, hope and love.

0 Res Mirabile! 0 Wondrous Thing!

The crowds walked away, but the Apostles - who were like very little children - did not. We must be very little children, and cling to our Mother Mary, who is ever inseparable from her Jesus, if we wish to remain faithful to this sublime truth of the Most Blessed Sacrament and Sacrifice of the Eucharist.

+

Really to believe in Jesus Christ is to believe in Him where He really is, in the Most Holy Eucharist. The Doctrine of the Eucharist is the critical Christian Doctrine. Everything turns, everything hinges on its acceptance or rejection.

Up to this point in the story of Christ's life, as we have said, all has been triumphant expansion. There has been hostility and opposition from the Pharisees, but so far it has been powerless. From now on, little by little but ever increasingly, the tide will turn.

Crowds will still follow Jesus, but they will be a little less numerous, a little less enthusiastic. Soon He will begin to speak of His coming suffering, His crucifixion and death. Soon He will enter on His final steadfast journey toward Jerusalem and the end. It will not happen all at once. It will take a good while. But the die has been cast. The course has been plotted. The drama has only to work itself out in the concrete events of the subsequent period.

"Haven't I chosen all Twelve of you? Yet one of you is a devil." And we too can become devils, if we do not pray. We too can drift away, "little by little," as St. Bernard said, toward the deadly sin of infidelity. We too can betray Jesus Christ, for we have free will, and must have it in order to love. Yet there is peace for us in Mary, the Mother of God and our Heavenly Mother, "the grace of Christ the Redeemer," by which He saves us from hell and confirms us in fidelity to Himself here in this greatest of the sacraments. Mary and the Eucharist always go together, simply because Jesus and Mary are always inseparable, and the Eucharist is Jesus.

But we must pray the Most Holy Rosary of our Virgin Mother, our Blessed and Beautiful Queen. We must pray very much for final fidelity, final perseverance in the fullness of faith and love, to her who is Christ's Mother and our only hope under Him. Mary is our only sure hope of final fidelity to Jesus in this Sacrament. It is her Holy Rosary only that ultimately binds us to our Eucharistic God.

All this is more than ever true today, when our contemporary world exists as almost nothing but one big, blatant, almost irresistible invitation to universal infidelity. Religion is absurd. Prayer is a waste of energy. Faith is superstition. "Luv, luv, luv" - or in other words, lust, greed, and self-satisfaction of any and every kind - this is all that's real.

But Mary, our truly Blessed Mother, says to us, "No! Jesus is most real here in the Eucharistic Sacrament and Sacrifice of His love and fidelity. Keep coming to me, and every time I will lead you past all the deceitful allurements of an empty world back to quiet, confident prayer here before His Holy Presence in the Blessed Sacrament. Trust in me to keep you faithful to Him. I can do it, and I will do it. I am His Mother and yours. I will unite you in perfect love."

+

"No one can come to me unless he is enabled to do so by my Father." To these words of Jesus we might add these others: "And no one can remain with me where I really am, in the Eucharist, unless he or she is enabled to do so by my Mother, Mary."

For surely it is the truth. For there are degrees of fidelity. They range from the bare minimum to the maximum of the great saints. One of the greatest of the saints, Bernard of Clairvaux, said that God has wished us to have everything -"the whole," *totum* - through Mary. This includes the grace and gift of final fidelity to Jesus here in the Eucharist.

Mary has been called "the true Enabler." She enables us to "keep going" along the path of progress, toward final victory over all sin and every weakness. She enables us to remain with Jesus, to "abide" in Him, to live on in His love, to keep growing in faith and fidelity to His Sacred Heart, here in this Sacrament. Mary keeps us faithful. She strengthens our wills, little by little, ever more and more.

Father Pierre Teilhard de Chardin spoke of "purity, faith and fidelity" as the "operatives," the "operative" virtues - the virtues that enable us to act. Faith and chastity go together, as St. Thomas Aquinas, the Eucharistic Doctor, has taught us, following St. Peter closely. Faith purifies the heart. Mary, the Woman of Faith *par excellence*, purifies our hearts, slowly but surely, if we pray to her. She makes us worthy to come to Jesus in this Sacrament. She keeps us coming to Him until the habit of perfect fidelity is formed in our souls, in our hearts, in our wills.

We cannot remain perfectly faithful to Jesus Christ where He really is, in this Sacrament, without entire and complete dependence on Mary, our Perfect and Perpetual Virgin Mother. For this Sacrament, above all others, is the Sacrament of Purity. We call it the Holy Eucharist. "Be holy, you who handle the vessels of the Lord." Be holy, you who approach so closely, so intimately, to the Holy God, and are united to Him in Mystical Eucharistic Communion.

Be pure. Be chaste. Be "Marian," in order to be truly and fully Christian, Catholic, faithful.

We cannot remain faithful all our lives to the True and Holy Cross of Jesus Christ unless we cling as little children to Mary, His Mother and ours, who alone stood there, weeping but absolutely and utterly faithful to the very end.

We cannot understand the real meaning of the Resurrection if we do not persevere with Mary our Mother through the "dark night" of crucifixion faith and fidelity to victory beyond suffering. We cannot reign with Christ if we refuse to suffer faithfully with Him. If we are unfaithful to Him, if we deny Him in this Sacrament, He will deny us.

But even if we are unfaithful, He remains faithful. For He is Fidelity itself, and He cannot deny His own Being, His own Nature as Truth, what He is substantially. We are treacherous sinners, and for this very reason the Crucified and Risen Jesus gives us Mary, His own Mother and ours, to bring us back, if necessary, and help us to begin again to walk in the way of final and victorious fidelity: "Child, there is your Mother!"

+

Monsignor Ronald Knox somewhere in his writings remarks about a certain "Demas," companion of St. Paul, whom we hear of in one of the Apostle's letters, only to read in a later letter that "Demas has deserted me, fallen in love with the present world."

It is very easy to "fall in love with the present world."

It is very easy to fall from real faith in Jesus Christ. It is very easy to drift away from strong, living faith in His Eucharistic Presence and turn to the things of a more cheaply, easily satisfying world.

It is very easy to be unfaithful. It is very easy to turn away.

And it can be very hard to come back. Sometimes it can be nearly impossible.

O Mary! Mother of God! How we need you! O Jesus, have mercy on us all! The world is so much with us, prayer is so spiritual, religion and faith seem so unsubstantial at times, so difficult.

O God of Fidelity! O Faithful Virgin Mary! Help us!

We must pray. We must begin again every day of our lives to return to prayer, to "Eucharistic" and Marian prayer.

We must be grateful for the Eucharistic Gift. We must say "Thank You!" to the Father of Our Lord Jesus Christ every single day of our lives by attendance at Mass and reception of Holy Communion if it is at all reasonably possible.

O God our Father, thank You for the Gift of Jesus in this Sacrament. O Lord Jesus Christ, thank You for the priceless Gift of Yourself in the Most Blessed Eucharist.

We pray for the gift of fidelity, of strong and enduring Eucharistic Faith. We make our prayer humbly, full of the gift of the fear of the Lord, yet full of joyful confidence that You, Lord Jesus, and you, Mary, our Mother, will protect all your children from the attractiveness of the easier way.

For surely there should be joy for us in this great Sacrament. "God is with us," here in the Eucharist in the fullest possible way. He is our Peace, here above all.

O Lord of the Eucharist, give us joy in fidelity, "joy in the truth" - that having given us so much, this much, You will not fail to give us, together with this tremendous Gift of Your own Divine and Human Self, all things else.

Quomodo non etiam cum illo omnia nobis donavit? How can it possibly be that God, who has given us in this Most Blessed Sacrament His own Crucified and Risen Son, will not give us - has not already given us, in principle - every other grace necessary for our salvation and sanctification?

Truly, because of the Eucharist, we are not lacking in any gift of grace. *Nihil vobis desit in ulla gratia*, as Dom Columba Marmion loved to quote St. Paul. And most of all, we have in Mary our Mother, "the grace of Christ the Redeemer," as Pope Paul VI called her, the sure pledge of our ultimate fidelity and the final victory of our faith.

Part Three

Integrity

VIII

You Are the Christ, the Son of the Living God

St. John remarks that at this time Jesus was going about in Galilee, "for He did not wish to go about Judea, because the Jews were seeking to put Him to death."

Yet the Pharisees and Scribes pursued Him even in Galilee. St. Mark says about this time that some of them came from Jerusalem and gathered about Him and managed to find fault with some of His disciples - this time for eating bread without first washing their hands. Jesus replied that it's not what goes into a person that defiles him, but what comes out of him. "The things that proceed out of the mouth come from the heart, and it is they that defile a person....evil thoughts, adulteries, immorality, murders, thefts, covetousness, wickedness, deceit, shamelessness, jealousy, blasphemy, pride, foolishness. These are the things that defile a person. But to eat with unwashed hands does not defile anyone."

So Jesus withdrew even further and "retired to the district of Tyre and Sidon," where He healed the daughter of that wonderful Canaanite woman who argued with Him, "Lord, even the little dogs eat the crumbs that fall from their masters' tables!" and won His exclamation, "O woman, great is your faith! Let it be done to you as you will."

He passed on to the region of the "Ten Cities" east of the Jordan, and then returned to the Sea of Galilee, where He healed many and fed the four thousand miraculously.

But the Pharisees and Sadducees came to Him again, St Matthew says, "to test Him," as usual. They asked him "to show them a sign from Heaven," Him who had already shown them innumerable signs. He called them to their faces "an evil and adulterous generation" and told them no sign would be given them, but only "the Sign of Jonas." Just as Jonas was in the belly of the whale "three days and three nights, so will the Son of Man be three days and three nights in the heart of the earth."

He Himself was the Sign, "a Greater than Jonas," at whose preaching the Ninevites had repented, and likewise "a Greater than Solomon," to hear whose wisdom "the Queen of the South" had come from the ends of the earth.

Then He left them, "and getting into the boat, crossed the sea." He warned His disciples, "Beware of the leaven of the Pharisees and Sadducees." And in the end they understood "that He was telling them to beware not of the leaven of bread, but of the teaching of the Pharisees and Sadducess."

At Bethsaida Jesus healed a blind man, in stages. Then they went on to the villages of Caesarea Philippi. As they were walking along, He asked His disciples, "Who do people say I am?" They answered, "Some say John the Baptizer, others, Elijah, others Jeremiah or one of the prophets." He said to them, "But who do you say I am?" Peter answered, "You are the Christ, the Son of the Living

God!"

Then Jesus said to them, "Blessed are you, Simon, son of John, for flesh and blood has not revealed this to you, but my Father in Heaven. And I say to you, you are Peter, and upon this Rock I will build my Church, and the gates of hell shall not prevail against it. And I will give you the keys of the Kingdom of Heaven, and whatever you shall bind on earth shall be bound in Heaven, and whatever you shall loose on earth shall be loosed in Heaven."

"Then," St. Matthew concludes, "He strictly charged His disciples to tell no one that He was Jesus, the Christ."

+

Sometimes we go back to the Hebrew "Messiah," and sometimes we prefer to use the Greek, "the Christ." In either case, the word means "the Anointed One." Jesus was anointed by the Holy Spirit at His very conception in the womb of Mary. His humanness was anointed by the Divinity for the mission, the task of redeeming and saving mankind.

Peter, the blessed Peter, was the one chosen by God to profess for us all this our faith in Jesus Christ, "the Son of the Living God." Christ is the Rock, Peter is the Rock, the Pope is the Rock. Peter is Jesus, and the Pope is Peter. This is our blessed faith, the faith of blessed Peter, <u>the</u> Apostle, Prince of all the Apostles.

Peter would suffer much for this faith. He would fail, and then rise again victorious. After Christ's Resurrection, He would ask Peter, "Do you love me more than these others? And Peter could and would answer truthfully, "Yes,

Lord...."

I marvel at the "hidden" greatness of Peter. Paul's greatness is obvious. Peter we are somewhat inclined to dismiss as marvelously wholehearted, loving, sincere, but when the chips were down - weak. Yet it was easier to be Paul than it was to be Peter. It was easier to be John. It was easier to be any other of the Apostles than it was to be the Chief - on whose heart lay the burden of the whole Church.

It was not so much tears of repentance that wore grooves into Peter's cheeks, but tears of repentant love. The heart of Peter is a profound Mystery of Love. We who are weak and sinful in the Church understand God's wisdom in making Peter her Visible Head - and we understand Peter's greatness. Who was humiliated and humbled as Peter was humiliated and humbled? Who loved as Peter loved? Peter is to be ranked with Mary Magdalen and John the Baptist. Peter's greatness lay in a love so repentant that it could not bear the comparative luxury of being crucified right side up, but chose instead the frightfully dizzying crucifixion upside down of one who knew He was not worthy of His Lord and Master, and was determined to be true to this knowledge. It was the path of utter humility and perfect love followed all the way to a simply glorious finish.

+

"You are the Christ, the Son of the Living God." You are He who was to come into the world. You are "the Redeemer of Man," the Savior of the world. Like Martha and the people of Sichar in Samaria, Peter made his confession of faith. But He went more accurately to the essence of

Christ's nature as Anointed Son of God, not stopping at His role in this world as Savior.

And here we might do well to meditate for awhile on the Divinity of Jesus Christ, that Peter had so wonderfully acknowledged.

Throughout history heresies have attacked this Divinity far more frequently than they have His humanity, His human nature. It is, in a sense, much more obvious that Jesus is human, a Man like us.

Yet that He is Divine is also abundantly clear. The course of His life in this world is filled with miraculous "signs" that only sheer blindness cannot see to be such. The final "sign" was the miracle of his Resurrection from death - but then there followed the wonderful "supplementary" sign of the Holy Spirit's presence in the Church herself.

Jesus Christ is truly God and truly Man. He is a Divine Person with a Divine Nature and a Human Nature. He is a God who has become human, not by ceasing to be Divine, but by "assuming" our humanness to Himself. He is "of one substance" with the Father in His Divinity and "of one substance" with us in His humanness. He took His human nature from the Virgin Mary by the power of the Divine Holy Spirit - He who is from all Eternity the Divine Word of God, the Only Son of the Father.

Jesus is the God-Man. He could not have died, even as Man, unless He positively willed to let the work of His executioners have its natural effect, the death of His body. In this lay His priestly Sacrifice for sin on the altar of the Cross. "He was offered up because He willed it." He said, "No one takes my life from me. I lay it down freely." And as one last demonstration of His power, when He was being sought for arrest in the Garden Holy Thursday night and answered His persecutors, "I am He," Scripture records faithfully that they all "drew back and fell to the ground."

O God of Power, O Lord Jesus, protect our faith in You, our precious gift of faith in Your Divinity. Protect Peter, the Pope, our Holy Father, that He may always be strong in the defense and profession of the Truth. Make us and keep us all humble and faithful.

O Lord Jesus, "You are the Christ, the Son of the Living God." We believe it with our whole being, with all that we are, with every fiber of body and soul. Confirm us in our faith. Confirm us in fidelity to the truth. Flesh and blood has not taught us, but the wonderful Holy Spirit of Your Father. True God and True Man, we adore You. Amen.

+

"You are the Christ, the Son of the Living God." Peter had said earlier, "We have come to believe and to know that You are the Christ, the Son of God." Peter believed it, but he also knew it. They all knew it - by faith, but as a deep conviction. Yet until the Holy Spirit "confirmed" them on Pentecost, they would remain weak in the virtue of fidelity.

We are confirmed - if we have received that sacrament - and even so we often remain even weaker. We do not correspond with grace. Yet the sacramental character of Confirmation remains, as the source of ever new graces, and finally, perhaps only after many years of weakness and failure, the Holy Spirit has His way with us - and we begin really to believe.

"You are the Christ, the Son of the Living God." You are the God-Man. We believe it, Lord Jesus. We have come to know it, by faith surely, yet as a strong and deep conviction. Yet our strength is nothing without Your grace, without the steady stream, the steady flow of Your graces and gifts of fidelity into our poor, wavering human hearts and souls.

We believe it. We know it. Yet of ourselves we remain weak, and dependent on continual prayer.

We believe that You are the Son of God. This faith of ours has conquered the world. Yet more than all this, we believe in You, we trust in You, we hope in You, we depend on You for the power to be and remain faithful.

O Lord Jesus, You are the Living Son of the Living God. Since Your Resurrection we seek You no longer "among the dead." You live in the Eucharist and in our hearts, in our faith and love. We find You in Your saving grace, in Mary, Your Mother and ours - and we depend on You there, in her Immaculate Heart.

Through her, through Mary, You keep us faithful to Yourself.

"To believe and to know" - both are so very important. Father Teilhard de Chardin rightly said, "It is so blessed to know!" If our faith does not really know, it will not survive. We know by faith, but we truly do know. And we must know. If we do not really know, our faith is not mature, not solid, not strong - even perhaps in danger.

Living faith is real knowledge. St. Peter is strong on this point: "Grow in grace and in the knowledge of Christ." But it is living knowledge, the knowledge of love, the

Biblical "knowledge of God," not the dead knowledge of "theologians" who don't pray.

It is only in prayer that we acquire this living knowledge of the Faith. It is only in prayerful meditation that we begin not merely to "know" the truth or "understand" it, but to savor it, to taste it by connaturality, and to hold it ever more firmly with the will. "Faith is the substance of the things we must hope for, a conviction about things we cannot see." As Peter said, "We have come to believe and to know."

+

Peter said to Jesus, "You are the Christ, the Son of the Living God." And Jesus said to Peter, "You are the Rock, and on this Rock I will build my Church."

This relationship between Jesus and Peter was unique. It was a mystery of love and trust, faith and confidence. It was a very beautiful mystery of friendship and childhood.

Jesus knew Peter, knew all his abysmal weakness, and loved him with an altogether special love. St. John rightly gloried in being "the disciple whom Jesus loved." But Jesus loved Peter even more, for Peter was "the disciple who loved Jesus." Whatever his great faults may have been, Peter was absolutely wholehearted with a wholeheartedness that was one of the most wonderful realities in the whole history of the world.

Peter was foolish. He was not wise. And what real lover is wise? Peter was a lover. He had much to learn, much humility, in order to mercifully teach it to all of us proud and petty people. Peter was not petty. He had a great big heart. He was foolish, but that is always the first stage of great love, real love, perfect love.

Peter was foolish, but he was not a fool. Or if he was, it was in the sublime sense in which he could have said even more truly than the great Paul, "We are fools for Christ!" Peter has taught us all not to be afraid to look and even to be foolish for the love of Jesus Christ. It is only the foolish who are truly wise with the wisdom of love. It is only those who dare to be fools for love who will ever finally come to learn "the Wisdom of God," the wisdom of him who is Truth.

Peter was a glorious fool. He was a coward, just like all the rest of us - without the grace of God. But his heart! His heart was in the right place - with a vengeance! He never calculated. He never sat back wisely and coldly and calculated whether he would possess of himself the strength to be faithful to Jesus. He loved, and He knew whom and what he loved, and he knew he would be faithful, by the ultimate power of Him who loved him in return, who he knew had loved him first. Peter had much humility to learn, but in the end he really was the most faithful of all the Twelve.

Peter is glorious! I love him! In him I see the magnificent heart that I for one have always been too petty, too timid to be. Peter had an utterly wild confidence in Jesus! Deep down in his heart, deeper than consciousness, was the certain knowledge that Jesus would supply all he lacked. And it was true. Peter had much humility to learn - we have said it before, and it can well be said many times - but it was inevitable that he would sooner or later victoriously learn it, because his love was very great and most true.

His love was Jesus. There was no other.

O Peter! O Rock! Give me a heart like yours! Humble, yes, but above all, loving and confident, heroically humble, confident and loving. O Prince of the Apostles, make me an apostle of Jesus Christ. Amen.

+

"You are Peter, and upon this Rock I will build my Church." He was as yet a very undependable Rock. He would need the Holy Spirit's gift of confirmation.

And even then, in fact, ever after his fall, in the light of his own self knowledge, and in the face of the obvious greatness of Paul, he would be diffident, with a tendency to yield to the judgment of others. Perhaps he would never lose this diffidence.

Yet in the end he would choose, with humble but iron decision, crucifixion upside down.

Peter was a success. For a long time he traveled the way of failure. He knew what it was to get a stinging rebuke on more than one occasion. Yet he always came back for more. It was the blind, unseeing, utterly confident love within his heart, a love that in the end would be absolutely victorious.

It was and remained always repentant love, love that "went out and wept bitterly," love that throughout the years and decades that followed shed streams of tears down his cheeks until they wore grooves of love in his very face.

Peter was to be a Rock like Jesus, a Rock with a human heart, a Rock who could image the very mercy of God, as one who had needed all of that mercy himself.

Christ's Church was to be a community of sinners. It was necessary that its visible head should have known the terrible weakness of sin and have triumphed over it by the special grace of God.

Peter, we kiss your foot. The millions of us kiss your foot. Help us triumph as you triumphed. Teach us to love as you loved, to believe as you believed, to be faithful in the end as you were magnificently faithful in the end.

Peter, help us. Give us big hearts like your own. Give us a profound and beautiful humility like your own.

O Prince of the Apostles, shepherd us! Keep us all safe for the Heart of Jesus.

O Jesus, God of the Rock, make us wholehearted as Peter was wholehearted. Make us true.

"I love You, O Lord, my Rock! O Lord, my Rock, my Fortress, my Deliverer!" O Savior of us all, make us rocks in the Rock. Make us humble witnesses of the Faith, diffident in the temptation to impose our personalities on others, patient in explaining as much as may be necessary, but finally, in the end, unyielding even to martyrdom, even to crucifixion, "inside out" or however it may be.

O Lord Jesus, O great St. Peter, make us Catholics, that we may live and die truly meriting to be called "the faithful." Amen.

+

"You are Peter, and on this Rock I will build my Church, and the gates of hell will not prevail against it...." Jesus asked in one of His parables on prayer, "Will the Son of Man find, do you think, faith on the earth when He comes?" Here He answers that question: The gates of hell shall not prevail against the Church, for He Himself is with us "all days, even to the consummation of the world." The Faith of the Church will endure even to the end of time - faith in the Eucharistic Presence of Jesus, faith in the Presence of His Holy Spirit among us all.

It is certain, but it is not "automatic." We must struggle to preserve and increase our own faith and to spread it to others. We must spread the victory of faith throughout the whole world. We must conquer the world by faith. We must believe and practice what we preach. We must pray.

We get discouraged, disillusioned, just plain tired. Well, then, let us rest - as much as we need to - and then let us return to work. "*Emmanuel*" means "God is with us," helping us to believe and to keep on moving forward toward the Kingdom of Heaven. As we advance, as we move forward along the way of faith and prayer, we will - not automatically, but certainly - draw many other human hearts along with us to their own victory in faith.

"This is the victory that overcomes the world, our faith." If this is so - and it is the very word of God - then the way of living faith is the way of victory, regardless of what it may feel like. The wise man does not live by feelings - only the fool does. Faith is in the intellect and the will. We know it's true. We only have to do it.

It is true that living faith is also somehow in the heart. It is connaturality with the Heart of Jesus and the Heart of Mary. But even if it does at certain times entail a sense of God's presence, it is still not a feeling, in the common, crass and even "carnal" sense of the word. It is a spiritual perception, but it is not emotionalism. Faith is not in man's sensibilities as temperance and fortitude are.

"Faith is the substance of the things we must hope for, a conviction about things we cannot see." By the grace of faith we possess now, even here on earth, the substance of the glory of Heaven, even though the experience may be seemingly almost non-existent, in dryness, aridity, emptiness, nothingness. Living faith is living knowledge of God, a deep and strong conviction about many things, many truths - the goodness, wisdom and power of the one true God, the Holy Trinity, the Incarnation, the Redemption, the Church, the Sacraments, the virtues and gifts - even on those days when we may feel little or no enthusiasm about it all.

By faith we see what cannot be seen, except by the power of the Holy Spirit. By faith we have spiritual light, the light of truth, in this dark world. By faith we are able to see the Kingdom that waits ahead of us. By faith we are able to keep walking toward it. By faith, in the power of this stupendous grace and gift, we will someday arrive. "Only believe!" Only believe with a strong, living, prayerful faith, and all is even now well. Let there be peace, even in obscurity and darkness.

+

St. Thomas Aquinas says that it is by faith in Jesus Christ that we make our first approach to God. Love should be the soul of this faith. And this faith itself should be the soul of Christian humility. These three virtues - humility, faith and love - embrace all the other virtues.

But faith is central. There is no living faith in Christ

without love for Him, but likewise there is no true humility - sign of genuine love - that is not impregnated by faith in Jesus, who said for us to learn humility from Him, and not to try to make ourselves humble in some other way. There is no other road to true humility than the following of Christ. And it is only faith in Jesus Christ that brings true love into the world.

But in a way, all these three virtues are simultaneous. Under the aspect of virtue, humility comes first. As grace, faith comes first. As gift, love comes first.

True faith is humble, living - loving - faith.

In the Gospels Peter appears as full of love for Jesus, and full of faith in a sense, but altogether lacking in humili ty and self-knowledge. This is the picture of many of us in the beginning.

Yet by the time he wrote his epistles, and even by Pentecost morning, what a difference! His faith has been confirmed and perfected, and his humility is a deep and quiet thing.

He tells us that although we do not see Jesus Christ, we love Him and believe in Him, and that the end of this way of faith will be an unspeakable and glorious joy in the final gift of salvation.

Peter has learned what it means to live by faith, to live in faith, to "keep going" in faith. And he is now able to teach us all. We sense his joy as he speaks of "the God and Father of our Lord Jesus Christ, who in His great mercy has given us a new birth to a living hope through the Resurrection of Jesus Christ from the dead...." As he goes on speaking of joy in tribulation, he makes us realize more and more how truly great is this "living hope."

St. Paul would say that "Christ is our Hope." For Peter, Christ is our Joy, in the deep certitude of faith.

Peter knows he has been forgiven. He knows whom he has loved. He knows that he is loved with a Divine Love that has washed him clean, cleansed the very deepest recesses of his heart and soul of all but a perfect and perfectly responsive love.

Peter has shown us the way. He has shown us sinners the way of repentance, confidence and love. He has shown us the way of victory, the way of heroic dependence on Jesus Christ by absolute faith. And now we too not only believe, but <u>know</u> - that our God is the God of miracles, who keeps His promises, and who can raise up children to Abraham out of the very stones on the ground.

+

Although we do not see Jesus, we love Him. Although we do not see Him, we believe in Him.

Certainly we do not see Him. Every morning at Mass we hold the Eucharist in our hand for a moment or two, and we make our act of fervent faith and love, and then consume it. It is the high point of our day. It is the most blessed moment of all the twenty-four hours. It is the moment when Jesus Christ, our Lord and our God, comes to us to unite Himself with us sacramentally, spiritually, mystically, totally, eternally more and more - to strengthen us and sustain us, to encourage us to keep hoping for and working toward sanctity.

Sometimes our faith may be very vivid, wonderfully full of life. Sometimes the joy may be very great.

But there are always days when we may experience little or nothing. We do not see Jesus. Yet we love Him and believe in Him.

Sometimes it may be almost as if we do see Him, by means of love. Sometimes our desire to be united to Him may be so powerful that we almost do seem to see Him in the quiet Mystery of the Consecrated Host.

Yet we do not really see Him. It is joy, it is love - and we may sometimes feel that it is perhaps "almost as good as vision." Perhaps we may call it the gift of true devotion, heartfelt devotion, earnest devotion, fervent devotion, zeal. If we do not see Him, perhaps there are times when it almost seems as if we don't need to. We know Him. We know He is present. He himself tells us so by the burning love and confidence He inspires within our breasts.

God comes to us, in Holy Eucharistic Communion. And we seem to see Him. For He strengthens our minds, He strengthens the eyes of our hearts, our eyes of faith. He enables us truly to believe, perfectly to love and hope - for a few precious moments at least.

By the grace of Jesus Christ, "truly, really and substantially" present in the Eucharist, we are enabled to believe with conviction. We are enabled to pray. And we gather up our whole world into our prayer, and we unite ourselves and all we love, all who are dear to us, everyone, to Jesus Christ in the moment of Eucharistic Communion.

The moment is sacred beyond words. The moments of Eucharistic Communion are the most blessed moments of our whole life in this valley of tears. They are moments worth living and waiting years or decades for. "One Holy Communion can make a saint." They may be moments worth waiting for for a whole lifetime.

They are the gift of prayer at its most wonderful and most holy. They are the moments that will make us what God wants us to be. They are the moments of love.

Even if we experience nothing.

O Lord Jesus, teach us always the prayer of living faith. Amen.

+

"You are the Christ, the Son of the Living God." You are the Divine Son of the Divine Father. You are the Eternal Word of the Eternal Speaker. To You we listen, to Him who speaks through You, who has spoken to us in You.

You are the Divine Image of the Infinite God. In You dwells all the fullness of the Godhead corporeally. In You are hidden all treasures of wisdom and knowledge. You are the Fullness of the Father. You fill the whole universe in all its parts.

You are the Anointed One who came into this world on a mission - "to destroy the works of the devil." You are the Good Shepherd, who came to bring a whole vast multitude of straying human sheep back to the fold of God.

You were anointed to save us all by suffering, and to teach us all likewise - each and every one of us - to take up our own individual Cross daily and follow You.

You have led the way. You have shown us the way. You Yourself have travelled first the Way of the Cross - and You have thus made it for us a way of hope, a way of faith and love, a way of resurrection as well as crucifixion.

O Lord Jesus, You are the Mystery of God, the Mystery

of the Father. You are in Your own Person the Mystery of the Father's love for us all. You bring us the Gift of His love in Your own Sacred Human Heart and in Your Holy Spirit.

You are the Messiah, the Christ, the Anointed One, the True Son of the Living God. We believe in You with the faith of Peter. We want to be living stones like him, the Rock, in the City of God, the New Jerusalem, the Church, now and forever.

In this world we are all being polished and perfected by one another, by trials and tribulations and troubles, in preparation for finding our eternal place as sparkling jewels in the Heavenly City.

O Lord, strengthen us! Make us faithful, and keep us faithful. We believe - help our unbelief!

You are the Anointed One. And You have anointed us too, with the Gift of Your Holy Spirit in Baptism and Confirmation. We are anointed to live Your life of grace, faith and love, to worship the Father through You, and to bring Your Holy Spirit and the Good News of Your Blessed and Eternal Kingdom to all we meet. We are anointed to bring this Holy Spirit to our whole world, to every nook and cranny of the world in which "we live and move and have our being."

But, Lord, we are poor, poor in humility, faith and love.

Strengthen us. Live in us. Speak through us. Save the world through us. Make us saints. Amen.

+

IX

He Was Transfigured Before Them

From the time of Peter's confession onward, "Jesus began to show His disciples that He must go to Jerusalem and suffer many things from the elders and Scribes and chief priests, and be put to death, and on the third day rise again."

St. Mark says, "What He said He spoke openly." And Peter was upset by it. He took Jesus aside and "began to chide Him" - "Far be it from You, Lord! This will never happen to You!"

Jesus turned, and eyeing the other disciples, rebuked Peter: "Out of my sight, you satan! You are thinking, not as God does, but as human beings do!"

Then He called together the crowd that had gathered and said to them all and to His disciples, "If anyone wants to come after me, let him deny himself and take up his Cross daily and follow me. For whoever will save his life will lose it, and whoever loses his life for my sake will save it.

He went on, "Whoever is ashamed of me and my words in this adulterous and sinful generation, of him will the Son of Man be ashamed when He comes with the holy angels in the glory of His Father. For the Son of Man is to come with His angels in the glory of His Father, and then He will render to everyone according to His conduct."

Then He concluded, "I tell you truly, there are some of those standing here who will not taste death till they have seen the Kingdom of God coming in power."

And then six days after these things, the Gospel says, He took Peter, James and John "and led them up a high mountain off by themselves and was transfigured before them. As He prayed, the appearance of His countenance was changed, and His clothing became a radiant white like snow, as no bleacher on earth can whiten." One account says that His face shone like the sun. Then two men appeared speaking with Him, "Moses and Elijah, who appearing in glory, spoke of the death He was to accomplish in Jerusalem."

Peter, James and John had fallen asleep, but woke up in the midst of all the glory. They saw Moses and Elijah, and as these were about to leave, Peter said to Jesus, "Master, it is good for us to be here! Let us set up three shelters, one for You, one for Moses and one for Elijah."

Actually, he didn't know what to say, it was all so astonishing and even frightening. But even as he was still speaking, suddenly "a bright cloud overshadowed them, and a voice out of the cloud said, 'This is my beloved Son in whom I am well pleased. Listen to Him.'" On hearing the voice the disciples fell on their faces with fear. Jesus came up and touched them and said to them, "Rise and don't be afraid." Then they looked up and saw no one but Jesus only.

As they were coming down from the mountain, "Jesus

cautioned them, 'Tell the vision to no one, till the Son of Man has risen from the dead.'" And St. Luke says that they "kept silence and told no one at that time any of these things that they had seen." They kept it all to themselves, but kept "discussing with one another what the words, 'When He shall have risen from the dead' might mean."

+

Pope St. Leo the Great says that Jesus gave Peter, James and John the experience of His Transfiguration so that the scandal of the Cross, when it came, would not totally destroy them. Perhaps if they had not had this experience to look back to, their failure would have been complete and permanent. At His crucifixion "all His disciples abandoned Him and fled." But perhaps it was because of this experience of the Transfiguration that the three leaders returned, and then the others with them.

In any case, Christ's Transfiguration is a great gift to us from Him through Peter, James and John. Peter looks back to it in his second epistle and tells us that the Apostles were not telling tall tales when they made known to us the power of the presence of Our Lord Jesus Christ, but they were witnesses of His greatness. For He received glory and honor from God the Father, when the voice came down to Him, "This is my beloved Son, in whom I am well pleased. Listen to Him." St. Peter says, "We heard this voice from Heaven when we were with Him on the holy mountain." Then he speaks of his even firmer "prophetic word" as a lamp shining in the darkness of this world. And such truly is Peter's powerful witness in all ages.

But Christ's Transfiguration takes place to some extent in the lives of all the saints. St. John of the Cross uses a slightly different word, "transformation," to express the spiritual reality, and speaks of "transforming union." Perfect love "transfigures" us, "transforms" us into Him to whom we are united by the grace and gift of holiness.

To put this into terms of "wholeness," we can say, using the language of St. Paul, "I live now, the sick man, no longer I, but Christ lives in me, the Whole Man." For this is surely the meaning of holiness and transformation into Christ, that He should, by the power of His grace, change us who are "sin-sick souls" into whole beings in Himself, into saints, healed spiritually and therefore through and through.

For what is the meaning of transformation into Christ if not to be made holy with His holiness and therefore also whole with His wholeness? For it is the simple truth that holiness is wholeness, and that wholeness is the root meaning of "integrity," which is in turn both a moral reality and in the saints a gift almost similar to the blessedness that Adam had before the fall, a faint reflection of the utter and total integrity of Jesus Himself as he moves forward toward crucifixion and resurrection.

+

The Transfiguration was a bit of Christ's eternal Glory refusing, for a few brief moments, to remain hidden beneath the cloak of His humanness. For in reality He is always our glorious Lord and God.

"He was transfigured before them." He let His native

Glory as God appear to His three chosen Apostles, that they might, as witnesses of it, confirm our faith in Him.

For even the splendor of His human appearance was to be almost totally eclipsed on the Cross, when "There was darkness over the whole land."

And not even after the Resurrection would Jesus show Himself to His followers in such splendor as He had on Mount Thabor.

It was a little bit of Heaven, and Peter could well exclaim, "Lord, it is good for us to be here!"

We experience the same thing ourselves, in the blessedness of prayer. And we are saddened when it passes and we have to return to ordinary life in this humdrum world. We want to stay and be with God in the happiness of mystical union, and it cannot be. We have life to live, work to do, struggles, and further victories to achieve.

Very little of our Christian lives is spent in the conscious experience of God. For the most part we live, not by experience, but by sheer, naked faith. Yet even this can be a wonderful thing, for St. John says, "This is the victory....our faith." Even when faith does not feel like victory, even when it does not seem like victory in any way, even at these times it nevertheless is and remains true and real victory. St. John says, "our faith," the living faith of the Church.

The moments of transfiguration come few and far between in our spiritual lives, but faith is always ready at hand. Faith is dependable - not always easy to live, but a solid, ever at hand virtue. We know the truth that Jesus is God, the God-Man, our Lord. We believe it, even without feeling it. We believe in Him, as St. Thomas Aquinas says, and this is our victory. We are victorious because He is victorious, and He is ours. "In the world you will have distress - but confidence! I have overcome the world!"

Christ has given us this victory called "our faith." We must only persevere in it by ever more and more constant prayer, till someday it is made definitive for us by a blessed, holy death. Our victory in faith will then become the blissful vision of Him who is now eternally transfigured in the Glory of His Kingdom. That Kingdom is ours, if only we persevere in the way of living faith. For the present it is called the Kingdom of God. For all who continue faithful to the end, into the End, through the end and into the Eternal Beginning, it will be called the Kingdom of Heaven.

+

The Transfiguration experience is a great gift. The older spiritual writers spoke of "consolation." Today we might speak more of encouragement. But it's all one - the gloriously wonderful experience of the presence of God, of His goodness and love.

Yet it comes and goes. But faith itself need not come and go. Faith is a permanent habit, a divine, "theological" virtue. We feel victorious in moments of profound union with God. But whether we feel it or not, we are and remain victorious as long as we go on believing in Jesus Christ.

"This is the victory....our faith." It is the victory that overcomes the world, the flesh and the devil, sex, drugs and alcohol, every moral deviation, if only we persevere. It is the victory that overcomes cowardice, failures in honesty and justice, sooner or later, if only we cling to Jesus Christ in prayer and in His sacraments. The way of faith can be a terrible way of the Cross, but it leads to victory even in this world, if only we persevere.

Visions are rare, even in the lives of the saints, and more and more rare in modern and contemporary times. The saints are really men and women and children of faith.

The only meaning of the Transfiguration of Jesus was to strengthen the faith of the Apostles. The meaning of "consolations" in the spiritual life is exactly the same, to strengthen us and enable us to bear the "desolations" that will inevitably follow.

Faith can be wonderful, all vibrant and glorious experience, but it is more often pure fidelity in darkness, emptiness, nothingness.

Yet fidelity is precisely the <u>fullness</u> of faith - "faith-fullness."

"Master, it is good for us to be here!" Sometimes we just love to pray. It's all so wonderful. Religion is such a blessed thing. The world has no attractions for us. It is easy to cling to "the good God."

But it's not always like this. Sometimes prayer is pure drudgery. Fidelity is a terrible thing. We almost feel like we can't go on living any longer. The world, the flesh and the devil seem extremely interesting. It is very hard to believe even in the existence of a good God at all.

Yet it may very well be at just such a moment that we attain to the reality of "transfiguration" or transformation or the fullness of union with God, and we are surprised, flabbergasted, to find ourselves faithful and victorious.

"This is the victory...our faith." If we persevere in believing, in praying, in fighting our way forward through the tears and the terrible confusion, to where we know

Jesus Christ really is waiting for us, victory will come.

+

"This is My beloved Son in whom I am well pleased. Listen to Him." The voice terrifies the Apostles, and they fall face down to the ground. Jesus says to them, "Rise, and don't be afraid."

This is really the main thing Jesus Christ has to say to all of us, to the whole world: "Don't be afraid." This is the Good News: The almighty, all powerful, awesome God love us and wishes us peace. He has sent His Divine Son not to condemn the sinful world, but to save it from all its sins - to save us, all of us sinners.

But this business of being saved can be scary. We are frightened nearly out of our wits by the holiness of this God and the consequent realization of our own sinfulness. Yet He says over and over again throughout the Gospel, "Confidence! Peace! Don't be afraid!"

We must believe in His goodness and love for us.

"Courage! Confidence! Peace! Don't be afraid!" We need to hear these words often. Even the sinless Virgin Mary needed to hear them from the lips of the Archangel Gabriel. And if she, how infinitely much more we pitiful sinners.

We are afraid. We live in darkness and ignorance. We cannot see very much, even by faith. We need God's words: *Nolite timere* - Don't be afraid.

"Do not be afraid, little flock, for it has pleased your Father to give you the Kingdom." We could never have earned it. It must come to us as a sheer gift of grace and glory, or it could never come to us at all. It comes as the Gift of the Father. It comes to us "in the very Person of Christ."

The strong God is all good - this is our hope and our great confidence. The Father Himself loves us.

We are afraid of our own powerlessness to win the Kingdom. We are afraid of our spiritual impotence. We are afraid of our weakness, our own treacherous selves. And Jesus says to us, "Don't be afraid. It's a Gift."

All is the gift of grace. All is love, and we thought we had to do so many other things. We thought we had to succeed. We thought we had to fight and win all our own battles. And Jesus says to us that victory is a gift, a gift of God's love.

We really thought we had to be God, in order to survive. And Jesus says, "Peace! Don't be afraid!" We were afraid to be children. And Jesus says, "Peace! It's okay to be little and weak and defenseless. It's okay to be a child."

+

God is our Father, and we are His children. "Be children in evil, and in mind mature." Yet the psychology of maturity can be overdone. Among all the children of God there must always survive a certain childlike simplicity that not only does not know evil, but that positively rejoices in the good.

Children are, for the most part, happy. They play. When we grow up, sometimes we stop playing. And this is not good. We lose the gift of happiness precisely when we lose the gift of childhood.

We have to make a living. We have work to do. We don't have time to play. Or if we do play, we "play" as adults "play," not as children, not as all the children of God should play, not as God's family.

Childlike faith is the only real faith. It is trust in the Father.

We are afraid to relax. "Thieves may break in and steal."

We do not live prayerful lives of religion and piety, because we do not have the confidence of children in God our Father.

We are afraid to forget about everything else and pray. We are afraid to abandon ourselves to the goodness and will of the Father.

Indeed, it might very well mean growing pains, and we are afraid to grow. We are afraid to grow spiritually, because it means becoming like little children and losing control of our lives.

We are afraid to trust.

We know that the Cross leads to the Resurrection. We may even realize that there is no other way to Resurrection and Life. Yet our fear of the Cross is greater than our confidence in Him who lays it on our shoulders. Our fear is greater than our love.

And Jesus says to us, "It is I. Don't be afraid."

The Cross of Christ means the love of Christ. The Way of the Cross is the road that leads to love's joy.

We have to remind ourselves, "This is the victory.... our faith."

When we believe in Him who lays the Cross on our shoulders, the Way of the Cross becomes a way of love.

Faith becomes confidence, and we experience it as victory. A little bit of the Resurrection comes into our lives, maybe not immediately, but soon enough, truly soon enough.

And we are grateful for having been privileged to suffer a little "for the name of Jesus." We say to Him with St. Therese of Lisieux that it is our joy "to have suffered like that, to have been a fool like that for Your sake."

+

In faith we meditate. In faith we push forward. In faith we "keep on keepin' on." We meditate on the life of Christ, on His public ministry, on His Transfiguration.

And lifting up our eyes we see that now there is no one else there, "only Jesus."

Our world was a crowded world. There was the government and every other kind of authority. There was our family, the whole seemingly endless tribe, and our friends, perhaps many, many of them. There was the world about us, a world of acquaintances, of people we scarcely knew, many of whom we have passed in the streets perhaps never to meet again. There were the people we read about in the newspapers and magazines and see on television. There were many, many people.

But now, lifting up our eyes, after the gift of transfiguration or transformation or fullness of union, we see "only Jesus." We see only Jesus in all this vast multitude, only Jesus in every human heart and soul, only Jesus - in authority, in family, in friends, in the world about us. Everywhere there is "only Jesus."

It is very good. It is the fullness of solitude. We are not

alone, far from alone. "*Emmanuel*" means "God is with us" - in Jesus Christ.

There really is nobody else. "Christ is all in each of you."

It is the blessedness of faith.

In faith we meditate, "our eyes fixed on Jesus, the Author and Finisher of our faith." There really is no one else in our field of vision now. He is all we can see.

It is the gift of faith. It is victory.

He gave us faith in the beginning. He has kept it growing in our hearts. And He will bring it to perfection.

It is Holy Faith. And we are confident that by the gift of grace, someday - at least in the last moments of our life - it will be perfect faith, filled with perfect love.

Even now there may be great love, even perhaps a relatively perfect love. For we can see "only Jesus" in everyone.

We are beginning to walk in the way of victory. We are walking with Jesus, with the Eucharistic Christ. In Him "we live and move and have our being." We live in His presence. We move forward, one step at a time, one day at a time, in the power of His nourishing gift. He Himself is the Gift. He is the Eucharist. He is our Strength, our Hope, our Power, our Truth, our All and our Everything. He is our Energy and our Living Faith.

+

He is our Grace, and He will be our Glory. He is our Light and will be forever. He is our Eternal Blessedness.

"To do right, that is the first step in the way of blessedness." And to follow this light of truth to the very end will mean that the last step in this way will be just like the first. Only hopefully it will be much more of a prayer, a prayer of perfect love in the fullness of faith.

"I am the Light of the world," Jesus says. "Whoever follows me does not walk in darkness, but will have the Light of Life." Jesus is the Living Light, the Light that is Life. In Him Light and Life are one.

In us it is not always so, but He is "the true Light that enlightens everyone who comes into the world." He enlightens us "to do right." To do what is right is to follow the way of truth. "To do right" is to follow the Light of Life.

St. Peter speaks of the power of Christ's presence. If we have faith, we can experience this power at any time, in our "visits to the Blessed Sacrament." And we may further say that Christ in the Eucharist is in a most real way "a Lamp shining in the darkness of this world."

It all depends on our faith. Our ability to experience the power of Christ's presence, our ability to see Him as a powerful Lamp shining in the darkness of our world - both depend on the strength of our faith.

We do not live in an age of faith. We live in an age of unbelief and despair. One is tempted to lament dismally that we live in an age of selfishness and lovelessness, together with hopelessness, but in reality these things are ultimately traceable to the universal lack of faith.

And faith is a gift that is given to much, much prayer. Therefore it would seem that the answer to all the world's problems is for us who believe, or claim to believe, to live up to our faith by leading lives of prayer.

We must meditate, and we must pray - and then the grace of God will descend from Heaven to transform our hopeless world into a civilization of good will and peace. If we truly believe in prayer, miracles of grace will come down in showers on this sick world we live in and are a part of.

The answer is prayer. The answer is meditation - which leads to prayer. The answer is to take time out every day for awhile to be quiet and still and try to think about the ultimate meaning of things. The Light and Love of God will come to meet us in the solitude and silence of our "quiet time." The grace and peace of God will come to our hearts as the gift of infused prayer. And that peace will go out from us to heal our whole environment - our neighborhood, our town, our country, our world. And all of us together will begin to walk in the way of blessedness.

+

We need to experience the power of Christ's presence. We need to experience His greatness. If our faith leads us to the Eucharist, it is because that is where the experience will sooner or later come to us. And the reason is simply that that is where Christ is to be found by us today. We will find Him nowhere else if we don't find Him in the Eucharist.

All His infinite greatness is contained in the little Host. And He can make us realize it, according to the greatness of our faith. If our faith is not at present great, let us pray. If we persevere in prayer, it will become great.

We persevere by beginning, again and again.

"To do right, that is the first step...." It is not right never to make the effort to turn our thoughts, our minds and hearts, to the God who made us, and the whole universe for our sakes. It is not right to give way to laziness and indifference and never get around to acknowledging Him as the tremendously "good God" that He really is.

The first step is to quiet down and be still, to stop running around in the endless pursuit of more and more "things." The first step is to stop and be still and open our eyes - or even close them if that will enable us to see better. The first step is to take a good long hard look at reality - to try and see it, perhaps really for the first time in one's life.

The world points to God, the world speaks of God, but it is possible to "look at" it for a whole lifetime and never really see it. To be still and try to see - this is the first step.

This does not mean staring at a tree for an hour in the effort to "see" its Creator. But it does mean seeing that a tree is a wonderful thing, something more wonderful than the world's greatest poet could ever produce - and that it does not owe its existence to any fool.

Philosophy began with the sense of wonder six centuries before Christ. In the middle ages it became "the handmaid of theology." And then theology lost the sense of wonder, and so it seems that we are in a way back where we started.

If we ever want to be even natural philosophers, human beings really, let alone theologians or mystics, we have to discover the world all over again - in all its wonder.

We have to sit down for awhile in the shade of that tree and be grateful for the protection from the midday heat. We have to be grateful for the marvellous little birds that make their nests in its branches, and then fly away when their young are hatched and reared. We have to be grateful for its multiplication in the forests that feed our need for mystery and beauty. We have to be grateful that it filters the sunshine into lovely streams that rest our eyes and raise them to the contemplation of . . .? dare we say God? Why not? If we are going to be grateful, and it makes so very much sense, why not be grateful to Him?

+

And if we say God, we must say Jesus. This is the power of His Resurrection.

For Christ has extended the power of the Tree beyond itself. The Tree has become for us the steppingstone to God. Christ climbed the Tree to rise beyond it to the Heavens. His body fell back down to the earth, but His soul rose upward. And then He took His body, with all the wounds it had carried on the Tree, and raised it up to the right hand of the Father.

We can reason to the Divinity of Christ. "Believe the works that I do." We can reason from His miracles, His "signs." But faith itself remains a gift which we cannot force on anyone. If one cannot believe, not even the supreme miracle, the sign of Christ's Resurrection, will make him believe.

The blind cannot see. Otherwise they would not be blind.

"But blessed are your eyes, for they see," said Jesus to the Apostles. Still, if we ourselves should claim to be able to see, we might merit Jesus' rebuke to the Pharisees, "If you were blind, you would have no sin. It is because you say, 'We see' that your sin remains."

So we must admit that we too are blind, even though we have the gift of faith and truly do believe. We do not seem to be completely blind, for we can see a little by this wonderful gift of faith. It is enough to enable us to keep walking forward through the darkness of this world toward the Kingdom of Heaven.

But surely it is our fault that we do not see more. If we had the faith of children, we would see all it is necessary to see. Let us be grateful that we can see this much - that God is our all good, all wise, all powerful Father, that Jesus is our all loving Savior, and that the wonderful Holy Spirit is our Friend, our Sanctifier, our "Lawyer." We can see the Church, the sacraments, and the truth that Mary is our Mother and Joseph our Protector from the devil, and all the saints and holy angels our big brothers and sisters, secure in their eternal victory.

By faith we can see enough. We can see the Glory of Jesus Christ in the Eucharistic Host, and from time to time in Holy Communion we can not only feel but also see that "it is good for us to be here" in Eucharistic union - so that when the moments of blessedness pass, our faith is strengthened to find Jesus Christ in all the moments of our day: in our difficult work, in our perhaps equally difficult neighbor, in our difficult perseverance in prayer.

We find Him in faith. This faith it is that is the victory that enables us to see Him who is the spiritual Light in the darkness of this world's reality. His Light is the Light of Truth and Goodness, shining amidst evil and error.

By the light of truth we choose the good, in faith, and it is another step forward along the way of blessedness, the way of victory.

X

He Set His Face Steadfastly Toward Jerusalem

Jesus went on teaching His disciples. He said to them, "The Son of Man will be betrayed into the hands of men, and they will kill Him. Having been killed, He will rise again on the third day." They didn't understand what He said, but they were afraid to ask Him about it.

Then it was autumn again. It seems that more than two years had passed since the summer when John the Baptizer had first begun preaching and baptizing at the Jordan.

The time was drawing near for Jesus "to be taken up from the earth," and "He set His face steadfastly toward Jerusalem."

The Feast of Tabernacles was at hand. His relatives told Jesus, "Leave here and go into Judea, so that Your disciples there too may see the things You do. Nobody does something in secret if he wants to be publicly known. If You do these things, manifest Yourself to the world." The evangelist remarks that not even His relatives believed in Him.

Jesus told them, "My time has not yet come, but your time is always at hand. The world cannot hate you, but it hates me, because I bear witness about it that its deeds are evil. You go up to the Feast. I'm not going up to this one.

My time is not yet at hand."

He stayed on in Galilee. But as soon as they had gone up to the Feast, "then He too went up, not publicly, but as it were privately." He left Galilee, it seems, for the last time, and started south for Jerusalem. It was late October. He passed through the heart of the Samaritan country, where He was not welcomed, because they could all tell He was a pilgrim on His way to the Temple.

+

In the next chapter we will tell the story, in the words of the Gospel, of what happens at the Feast of Tabernacles (or "shelters"), and then later we will consider the rest of Jesus' doings in Judea and Perea the last months of His life. But let us stop now and dwell for awhile on what St. Luke says about the time being near for Him "to be taken up from the earth," and His setting His face "steadfastly toward Jerusalem."

For all practical purposes He was through in Galilee. His work there was finished. He had spent much time there largely because the Pharisees made life so unpleasant for Him down south in Judea.

But He could do so no longer. Pharisees or no Pharisees, duty, His Father's will, was calling Him. Jesus was a Man of Peace. He did not like fighting hatred and wilful blindness. But now the time had come when He no longer had any choice. He must go to Jerusalem, to war and to death.

He "set His face." It took a stern effort of His human will. It would require all the power and strength of His

Manhood to deal with the "serpents" that were awaiting Him in the capital City.

He had come into the world "to destroy the works of the devil," and He had to begin by making one last long and toilsome effort to turn the hearts of these minions of the devil, lest they "die in their sin."

It was going to be very unpleasant, bitterly unpleasant. It was going to be exhausting. And it was going to end up largely in failure - and finally in His own death by crucifixion.

There was nothing to look forward to, except the relatively remote joy that lay beyond the Cross. Proximately, all was bitterness, tending even to extreme depression.

Yet St. Luke says, "He set His face steadfastly." He was a Man. He was the God-Man with work to do that only a God-Man could do. With His human mind He would be battling angelic intellects. With His human will He would be clinging to the will of His Father, which was to save people and not to destroy them. What saint, what other preacher would ever be purified by truth and love so painfully as Jesus Christ would preach truth and love so purely in these His last days on earth!

He made His decision. He made up His mind. He began to move south. He knew He was walking toward frustration, failure and death. But He was walking in the truth, and He would lead us all in the way that we too must follow in our lesser degree.

Immediately He met diabolical opposition in the form of Samaritan opposition. It seemed as if from now on almost everyone and everything would unite under the leadership of the evil spirits to oppose Him.

During these last few months of His life, all His forward progress would be made painfully, inch by inch, down a gauntlet of hatred and opposition, until it became a veritable *Via Dolorosa.*

Yet He had made up His mind. He had "set His face" - and He walked forward. He left Galilee, where the people had almost all acclaimed Him so enthusiastically, but whose cities had really accepted Him no more truly than would Jerusalem itself. His Heart was heavy, but His will was firm.

He was a Man. He was the God-Man. And He was Truth Itself.

+

We can learn a lot from the "steadfastness" of Jesus. "My heart is steadfast, O God, my heart is steadfast!" cries the Psalmist. And we can perhaps sense, or perhaps it is true of ourselves, that the words may be spoken through bitter tears and with a supreme effort of the will.

There are many times, and in our world of weakening moral principle they may be becoming even more and more frequent, when we must be steadfast.

Life may present us fairly often with hard things that just simply have to be done or endured.

And sooner or later, death itself begins to make its appearance on our spiritual horizon, and we "set our face steadfastly" to go forward to meet it, as God may will.

There was love in the Heart of Jesus as He moved forward. There was very great love for Jerusalem, Jerusalem that stoned the prophets and put to death all the messengers that were sent to her. He longed to gather her young under His wings as a hen does her chicks. But Jerusalem would not have it.

We must be careful lest we too become Jerusalem in this carnal and earthly sense.

We must pray for the gift of truth, the gift of responsive love.

We must communicate, at any price - and it may well mean crucifixion.

"Your house will be left to you, a house uninhabited." We too must heed these words. We must pray for eyes that can see and ears that can hear.

We must pray for a human heart. We must pray for the gift of understanding with the heart. We must simply pray, and persevere in prayer.

Our faith is our victory. The prayer of faith is the victory of faith. To be steadfast in faith and prayer - this is the victory. And it is a victory that must be won anew every day.

"My heart is steadfast, O God, my heart is steadfast. I will sing...." But often we may not really feel like singing, and this "steadfastness" of our heart is purely in the will.

We are so weak. And yet we struggle to be faithful, to be and to remain steadfast in faith and prayer.

We move forward. We will it. Like Jesus, we will to advance, to proceed, even if it means walking forward to death, even if it means walking on in darkness, without any feeling of hope.

It is unpleasant. We have to keep going without satisfaction. We look at Christ. We contemplate the God-Man, willing to move on down the road toward Jerusalem. We follow. In the strength of His grace and gift of faith we follow in seeming darkness, knowing only that He is there walking ahead of us, leading us all.

He will never turn around, until the final victory. We follow, for He is our Strength.

+

Can we imagine how much it must have cost Jesus to make this final decision to set out for Jerusalem, and the conflict with the Pharisees that would not let up again until He was crucified and dead? He loved them, and He was the Truth that could save them, and He knew they would not only not accept Him but would reject Him with all the power of their being. As the willing tools of the fallen angels they would crucify the Lord of Glory.

Let us look to ourselves. It is very easy to become a tool of the devil. It is very easy to slip and slide down the road of infidelity toward denial and betrayal of the Lord of Glory. One need only "go along" with "the world."

Actually, in our day it is extremely difficult not to go along with the world, with the crowd, one almost wants to say "with the community." The word of the Gospel is there: "How narrow the way that leads to life, and how few there are that find it!" The broad way is easy and enjoyable, and it seems so right. The narrow way of truth and virtue seems so lifeless, so stuffy, so foolish.

It is hard to pray. And even if it is not always hard, it is extremely hard to persevere in more and more prayer to the very end. It may be hard to begin, but then there come consolations. But later the consolations seem to come more and more rarely, and one feels so, so weak and tired of trying to communicate with this truly "hidden God." It seems so meaningless, so unreal.

We seek distractions. We wander away from the effort to meditate and pray. We are guilty of little - and sometimes perhaps not so awfully little - infidelities. We run low on energy.

And then we come back, ashamed of ourselves, and cry out for mercy. What has happened to all our ideals? We are growing old and it seems we are still not the saints we promised ourselves in our youth we would become.

We are growing old, and we are failures - so it seems - and we cry out in prayer to the God we know can make anything right, "My God, I love You! Have mercy on me a sinner!"

It is a prayer made in faith, and in faith the answer comes as a bit of firmness in our hearts and wills. We pray quietly, "Come, Lord Jesus!" And it brings us peace. But we know that we have work yet to do in this world, in this valley of tears.

And so we "set our face steadfastly" in faith, and it becomes a prayer, a new prayer that is the gift of Jesus to us. It is a return to prayer, a grace of renewed fidelity, a strengthening of the will, a strengthening of our hope, a reinvigoration of our old hope of sanctity, the hope that burned so strongly years or decades ago in our youth, and that Jesus Christ promises is not in vain.

+

The time was drawing near for Him "to be taken up

from the earth." First He would be lifted high on the Cross, and then after His Resurrection He would ascend victorious into Heaven. It was all an upward path.

He was the God-Man, but He had a job to do in the power of His human will. It would be incredibly hard. It was not play-acting. He was fully human, far more fully human than we are, perfectly human, perfectly sensitive to suffering because never hardened and dulled against it by sin.

We live our lives in a semi-consciousness, in a semi-darkness that is the result of all our moral compromises. Jesus and Mary knew no such darkness. They suffered what we have largely become inured against, even blind to, the profound falseness of the world.

Jesus' human will had a mission to fulfill. It is true that He could not fail, that He was omnipotent and impeccable, Divinely so. But the human suffering this mission would involve for Him! The incredible suffering! The endurance, pain, agony, desolation, anguish, distress! His Divinity only enabled Him to suffer in His human nature what no man would otherwise have been able to suffer, to endure, to bear, to sustain.

He suffered sin. It transformed Him into itself, on the level of disgust and wretchedness, on the conscious level of revulsion, nausea, torment. It was by the will of the Father. "For our sakes God made Him who did not know sin to be sin, that we might become the justice of God."

It was justice. It was right order working itself out by the willed plan of God. It had to be. It was the righting of all wrong. It had to be done - because God is Truth. God is Light, and sin is darkness. God's Light must triumph over the devil's darkness. A man had sinned, and after him many others. A Man must right all that wrong.

Jesus would do it, in the power of His Divinity, and in the infinite power of His humanness to suffer, and repair the injury done to justice, to right order, to truth, to love.

Jesus loved. He loved the Truth. He was the Truth of the Father. He chose obedience, sacrifice, death. He chose crucifixion as the only honorable road to resurrection and life. With His human will He chose to be true. He chose to give us a picture of God's love for us.

It is good to be true. It is good to choose life, even when it means apparent death. It is good to be faithful.

It is good for us to meditate on the utter fidelity of Jesus Christ. It is good for us to turn away from the deceitful world and pray to Him for the gift of union with Him, wherever He is going.

+

We are steadfast in prayer. There is "joy and peace in believing." It is the gift of Jesus, our reward for following this far.

We must continue to follow.

It is work.

All is still. All is calm and quiet faith. We are following Jesus Christ. We have only the vaguest idea of what lies ahead. Perhaps we have none at all. Our "Jerusalem" will probably be materially very different from His. We know only that Resurrection and Life lie beyond crucifixion and death.

He says to us, "You are the ones who have remained

with me in all my trials." We have come this far, and we are still with Him. We know that there came a time when the men to whom He first spoke those words "all abandoned Him and fled." We know ourselves. We know that we are no better.

We cling to His Mother, Mary, our own Mother and Queen of Peace. We are learning humility, and probably have much more to learn before we can say with St. Therese of Lisieux, "I have understood humility of heart." We ourselves seem to understand little or nothing - except the promise of Jesus, "Ask and you shall receive...." We understand that holiness, fidelity, is a grace and a gift.

We follow along the way of prayer and faith.

Christ inspires and inspirits us and makes us feel strong and full of hope. We know that feelings pass and are not to be depended on, that really, they mean nothing. Yet the experience of hope is good. He is our Hope.

He is our very great Hope. He is our Hope of sanctity, perfect love, spiritual success. He is our Hope of dying a blessed death like truly `honorable soldiers. He is our Hope, in fact, even of knighthood.

Sometimes we feel so very petty, miserable in our contemptible failure. But He is our joyful Hope.

We are learning to control the tongue, to be silent and pray, to remain little and hidden, to seek greatness where it is really to be found, in His meekness and humility.

We are learning to follow Him in reality, not just in the feeling of exaltation and happiness. We are learning wisdom. We are learning real life.

We are learning that the real "communication" is Eucharistic, that He is our Strength and Sustenance precisely in this magnificent Sacrament, that He is All and we are nothing, that He yearns to be our peace.

"Come to me," He says to us all, "all you who labor and are burdened. I will give you rest." We are learning that it really is true. We are learning where to find "rest for our souls."

+

There may be many times in our lives when we have to "set our face steadfastly" toward the next step leading to the Kingdom of Heaven. Then we have to take that step. We have to keep going - forward, always forward. God knows, it is not easy. We wonder, where will the strength, the energy, even the vision, come from?

Sometimes there seems to be no vision, only faith, in which we must and do step forward. And the Way is always there, opening out before us. Jesus has promised that it - He - always will be. In following Him we do not walk in darkness, but in the true light of true life, the living light of living faith.

We must keep going. Sometimes it doesn't seem that it will any longer be possible. But it is always possible. We have more strength, more energy in grace than we realize. What discourages us is that often we cannot see. But if we move forward in faith, the will draws our whole being, including the intellect, along with it, and we are enabled to see all we need to see for the moment.

We see that we must keep advancing, and that it is good to keep advancing, for the Kingdom of Heaven awaits us ahead. Indeed, it is nowhere but straight ahead, down the trail of progress and perseverance, straight ahead, down the road of faith and patience.

So like Jesus we keep on going. He is with us, supporting us, strengthening us, carrying us by the gifts of the Holy Spirit, and not least of all by the wonderful gift of fortitude.

How difficult it is! But we experience no difficulty that Jesus Christ has not already met and conquered for us, if only we go to Him and cling to Him in the dependence of faith. We have only to walk in the path of good deeds He has marked out for us as He Himself passed ahead.

All day long, from His Presence in the Eucharist, He sustains our faith and our fortitude. It is really a great privilege for us to walk our little Way of the Cross in the footsteps of so noble a Lover and Leader. It is a great privilege for us to struggle in union with Him against the same cosmic entropy that He fought and overcame.

It is a privilege we do not deserve, but He holds out to us, by His all powerful grace, the hope of a nobility in some sense worthy of His Human Heart, if we believe in Him and cling to Him and press forward, even heroically, along "the new and living way," the way of confidence and love, marked out for us by "the Seraph of Lisieux," after the pattern of great St. Paul.

+

"He set His face steadfastly...." He was quite simply determined. He intended to do it, no matter what. He had the power. He had the will, and He was exercising it.

He gives us too the power to "will it," to will to keep advancing toward the death of the body and eternal joy.

We can do it. We have the power, in His gift of grace. We must pray very much, but we have the power to pray, given us by the grace of faith.

We will do it. We have the victory in "our faith." This is not the devil's faith, dead, lifeless faith - but rather the living, loving, praying, suffering, struggling, Catholic, Apostolic Faith of Mary and Joseph, of John the Baptist and Mary Magdalen, of Peter and John and Paul and all the saints, the faith of the whole Church.

We have the intention. But this is really the intention to depend on God the whole way and to "draw our strength from the Lord." Jesus' human will drew its strength from His Divinity. We draw our strength from the Holy Spirit's gift of fortitude. "I can do all things in Him who strengthens me" - even become a saint, even the saint, the martyr, the apostle that God is calling me to be.

Humility may say in all truth, "I am nothing. I know nothing." But faith can add with even more truth, "I can do all things in Him who strengthens me."

Sanctity! Perfect charity! The perfect love of God! It may seem impossible - but it is not impossible. Pope John Paul II says it's a gift, and it is given to prayer. Heroic love is a gift, and it is given to much, much prayer. But much presupposes a little. Perseverance presupposes a beginning, and really consists in nothing more than a longer or shorter series of beginnings, over and over again.

All of us can begin. There is no one who cannot begin. And to pray once is to receive the grace to pray a second time. This is the path to victory, the way of "beginning." The perfect are simply those who began - and never quit beginning, never gave up, those who began and never stopped.

"He set His face steadfastly...." The Latin might be translated, "He firmed up His face...." The New American Bible translates the Greek as "He resolutely determined...." But neither of these has the power of the traditional English Catholic translation.

"He set His face...." He set it hard, like a Man who knew it was not going to be at all easy. "He set His face" against the whole of hell.

+

"I have a baptism with which to be baptized," Jesus said, "and how I am straitened until it be accomplished!... I have come to hurl fire on the earth, and what will I have but that it should flame out!... I have not come to bring peace, but the sword!..."

He would say to the Apostles, "It is my peace I give you." He does not give us just any kind of peace, but only His own unique peace - which is peace in the midst of fire and war, true peace, spiritual peace.

If we would follow Him the whole way, we must set our faces like concrete. We must become spiritual rocks, living stones, in order to be fit material for the Heavenly City.

"He set His face steadfastly," and then He started walking. There was no need to walk fast, only to keep moving steadily forward.

Jerusalem lay ahead, "the City of the Great King," and He was the Great King, and Jerusalem would reject Him. He is our King. Let us see that we do not reject Him, when

He comes to us in the modern day Jew, or the troubled woman, or the spoiled little child.

It is very easy to reject Jesus Christ. And sometimes it is very hard not to. He plays no favorites. He loves all mankind. His Church is not the community of the privileged, but a family of workers for the salvation of the whole world.

It is necessary to "set one's face steadfastly," and to do it again and again, daily, until the end. It is true that the way of living faith is the way of victory, but we may sometimes feel that this way of victory is "not all that it's cracked up to be." It is not a way of ease and comfort, but a way of truth - and the truth is that the victory is not complete and total until we are the saints God wants us to be, and safe in the Kingdom of Heaven.

But to have in one's heart the grace of living faith is to be victorious in principle and at least to some extent in practice. The peace of God will become stronger in our hearts after every step forward we take along the way.

The way of living faith, the way of victory, is the way of war with the devil, the way of struggle, work and suffering. It may not often be a way of exhilarating joy, but there will be times when one knows by experience that "God is on my side." And if God is for us, who can be against us? "Resist the devil, and he will flee from you."

We must set our faces "steadfastly" to resist - the whole way. This is the meaning of victory. To resist is to advance victoriously.

+

"He set His face steadfastly...." We too must be steadfast in faith. We too must set out "toward Jerusalem."

We must remember that this way of living faith along which we are walking, though not yet a way of complete and total and perfect victory, the victory of the saints in Heaven, is nevertheless a way of true and real victory.

The very fact that we feel nothing, except perhaps the difficulty of advancing, means that we are living by this victorious faith and not by feelings.

Jesus Christ was victorious from the first moment of His existence in this world, from the moment of His conception in the womb of Mary, His Mother, from the first moment of His Incarnation. More than this, He is eternally victorious. And we are victorious by our dependence on Him - heroic it may truly be - by His gift of grace.

We have the power to advance. By leading us He has won for us the grace to follow Him. He is our Eucharistic Leader even today, 2,000 years after Calvary and the Cross. If He leads us to our own Cross and Calvary, it is because it is good and necessary, and because in His infinite love for us He will provide us with the gift of fortitude in all its fullness, the fullness of the Holy Spirit, the Sanctifier.

Living faith, victorious faith, "our faith," is the faith of the original Apostles and of all true apostles.

Jerusalem awaits us. But ultimately it is not merely the Jerusalem that stones the prophets and murders the messengers that are sent to her, but beyond all this, the Heavenly Jerusalem, the Beautiful Spiritual Jerusalem of Resurrection and Life, Eternal Joy and Peace, Bliss forever in the Presence of God.

We can do it. Jesus did it first to show us how and to give us the power. We "set our faces," and we step forward.

The road stretches out ahead of us. We don't have to do it all in one day. We only have to keep moving forward, one step at a time, one moment at a time, one day at a time.

"This is the victory," to keep on going in faith. "Ask and you shall receive, seek and you shall find...." Surely we may add, "Advance and you will arrive."

XI

Before Abraham Came to Be, I AM

We have followed Jesus all through His public ministry. And now He is nearing the end of His mission. We have seen that end drawing near. Throughout this chapter, of confrontation with the Pharisees, we will simply let the Gospel text speak to us for itself. We cannot tell the story of these pages better in any other way. Let us be aware that to some extent at least it may be the story of our own spiritual blindness and hardness of heart.

It was the Feast of Tabernacles or "Shelters" in Jerusalem. The Jews were all looking for Jesus. They were asking, "Where is He?" There was a lot of whispered comment among the crowds about Him. Some said, "He's a good man." But others said, "No, He seduces the crowds." But for fear of the Jewish authorities no one spoke openly of Him.

Then when the Feast was about half over, Jesus appeared in the Temple teaching. They marvelled, "How does this man come by learning? He has never studied."

Jesus said, "My teaching is not my own, but His who sent me. If anyone desires to do His will, he will know whether my teaching is from God or whether I speak on my own authority. Whoever speaks on his own authority seeks his own glory. But whoever seeks the glory of the one who sent him is truthful, and there is no injustice in him. Did not Moses give you the Law? Yet none of you keeps the Law. Why do you seek to kill me?"

The crowd answered, "You have a devil! Who seeks to kill you?"

Jesus said, "One work I did, and you all wonder." (He had healed a man on the Sabbath.) "Moses gave you circumcision - not that it comes from Moses but from the fathers - and even on a Sabbath you circumcise a man. If a man can be circumcised on the Sabbath that the Law of Moses may not be broken, are you indignant with me because I made a whole man well on a Sabbath? Don't judge by appearances. Judge honestly."

They wanted to seize Him, but no one laid hands on Him, because, as the Gospel says, "His time had not yet come." Many of the people, though, believed in Him, and they kept saying, "When the Christ comes, will He work more signs than this Man works?" The Pharisees heard the crowds whispering these things about Him. Finally, they and the Jewish rulers sent men to seize Him.

Jesus said, "Yet a little while I am with you, and then I go to Him who sent me. You will seek me and will not find me. And where I am you cannot come." The Jews said among themselves, "Where is He going, that we shall not find Him? Will He go to those dispersed among the Gentiles and teach the Gentiles? What is the meaning of this statement that He has made, 'You will seek me and will not find me, and where I am you cannot come'?"

Then on the last day, the great day of the feast, Jesus

stood and cried out, "If anyone thirst, let him come to me and drink! For him who believes in me, as the Scripture says, 'Out of His Heart shall flow rivers of living water.'" He meant the Holy Spirit, whom those who believed in Him would receive. For the Holy Spirit had not yet been given, for Jesus had not yet been glorified.

When they heard these words, some of the crowd said, "This is really the Prophet!" Others said, "This is the Christ!" But some were saying, "Can the Christ come from Galilee? Doesn't the Scripture say that it is of the offspring of David, and from Bethlehem, the village where David lived, that the Christ is to come?" They were divided. The men wanted to seize Him, but did not lay hands on Him.

They returned to the chief priests and Pharisees, who said to them, "Why haven't you brought Him?" They answered, "Never has man spoken as this man!" The Pharisees retorted, "Have you been led astray too? Has any of the chief priests believed in Him, or any of the Pharisees? But this crowd, which does not know the Law, is accursed."

Nicodemus, who had come to Him at night, and who was one of them, said, "Does our Law judge a man without first giving him a hearing, and knowing what he does?" They answered, "Are you a Galilean too? Search the Scriptures. No prophet comes from Galilee." That evening they returned each one to his own house. But Jesus went to the Mount of Olives and spent the night there.

At daybreak He came again into the Temple. All the people came to Him. He sat down and began to teach them.

The Scribes and pharisees brought a woman caught in adultery. They stood her out in the middle and said to Him,

"Master, this woman has just now been caught in adultery. In the Law Moses commanded us to stone such persons. What do you say?" They said this to test Him, in order to be able to accuse Him. But Jesus stooped down and began to write with His finger on the ground.

When they continued asking Him, He raised Himself and said to them, "Let him who is without sin among you be the first to cast a stone at her." Then He stooped down again and began to write on the ground. Hearing this, they went away, one by one, beginning with the eldest. Jesus remained alone, with the woman standing out in the middle.

Jesus raised Himself and said to her, "Woman, where are they? Has no one condemned you?" She said, "No one, Lord." Then Jesus said, "Neither will I condemn you. Go your way, and from now on sin no more."

Again, therefore, Jesus spoke to them, "I am the Light of the world. Whoever follows me does not walk in darkness but will have the light of life." The Pharisees said to Him, "You bear witness to Yourself. Your witness is not true."

Jesus answered, "Even if I bear witness to myself, my witness is true, because I know where I came from and where I am going. But you do not know where I came from or where I am going. You judge according to the flesh, I judge no one. And even if I do judge, my judgment is true because I am not alone, but He who sent me is with me, the Father. And in your Law it is written that the witness of two persons is true. I bear witness to myself, and the Father who sent me bears witness to me."

They said to Him, "Where is your Father?" Jesus

answered, "You know neither me nor my Father. If you knew me you would know my Father too."

He said to them, "I am going away, and you will seek me, and you will die in your sin. Where I am going you cannot come." The Jews therefore kept saying, "Will He kill Himself, since He says, 'Where I am going you cannot come'?"

He said to them, "You are from below, I am from above. You are of this world, I am not of this world. That's why I said to you that you will die in your sins. For if you do not believe that I am He, you will die in your sin."

They said to him, "Who are you?" Jesus answered, "The Beginning, who am even now speaking to you. I have many things to speak and to judge about you. But He who sent me is true, and the things I heard from Him, these I speak in the world." They did not understand that He was speaking to them about the Father.

Jesus said to them, "When you have lifted up the Son of Man, then you will know that I am He, and that I do nothing of myself. But even as the Father has taught me, I speak these things. He who sent me is with me. He has not left me alone, because I do always the things that please Him."

When He was speaking these things, many believed in Him. Jesus therefore said to the Jews who had come to believe in Him, "If you abide in my word, you shall be my disciples indeed, and you shall know the truth, and the truth will make you free."

The Jews who did not believe answered Him, "We are the children of Abraham, and we have never yet been slaves to any one. How can You say, 'You shall be free'?"

Jesus answered them, "I tell you the truth, everyone who commits sin is a slave of sin. But the slave does not remain in the house permanently. The son does. If therefore the Son makes you free, you will be free indeed. I know that you are the children of Abraham, but you seek to kill me because my word takes no hold among you. I speak what I have seen with the Father, and you do what you have seen with your father."

They answered, "Abraham is our father." Jesus said to them, "If you are the children of Abraham, do the things Abraham did. But as it is, you are trying to kill me, a man who has spoken the truth to you which I have heard from God. This Abraham did not do. You are doing what your father does." They said to Him, "We have not been born of fornication! We have one Father, God!"

Jesus said to them, "If God were your Father, you would surely love me. For I came out from God and have come from Him. I have not come of myself, but He sent me. Why don't you understand what I say? Because you cannot listen to my word. Your father is the devil, and you will to do what he desires. He was a murderer from the beginning and has not stood in the truth because there is no truth in him. When he tells a lie he speaks from his very nature, for he is a liar and the father of lies. But because I speak the truth you do not believe me. Which of you can convict me of sin? Whoever is of God hears the words of God. The reason why you do not hear is that you are not of God."

The Jews answered, "Aren't we right in saying that you're a Samaritan and have a devil?" Jesus answered, "I don't have a devil, but I honor my Father, and you dishonor me. Yet I do not seek my own glory. There is One who seeks and who judges. I tell you the truth, if anyone keep my word, he will never see death."

The Jews said, "Now we know that you have a devil. Abraham is dead, and the prophets, and you say, 'If anyone keep my word he will never taste death.' Are you greater than our father Abraham, who is dead? And the prophets are dead. Whom do you make yourself?"

Jesus answered, "If I glorify myself, my glory is nothing. It is my Father who glorifies me, of whom you say that He is your God. And you do not know Him, but I know Him. And if I say that I don't know Him, I'll be like you, a liar. But I know Him, and I keep His word. Abraham your father rejoiced that he was to see my day. He saw it and was glad."

The Jews said to Him, "You aren't yet fifty years old, and have you seen Abraham?"

Jesus said to them, "I tell you the truth, before Abraham came to be, I AM."

So they took up stones to throw at Him, but Jesus hid Himself and went out from the Temple.

As He was walking along He saw a man blind from birth, and His disciples asked Him, "Rabbi, who has sinned, this man or his parents, that he should be born blind?" Jesus answered, "Neither has this man sinned, nor his parents, but the works of God were to be made manifest in him. I must do the works of Him who sent me while it is day. Night is coming, when no one can work. As long as I am in the world I am the light of the world." Having said this, He spat on the ground and made clay with the spittle and spread the clay over the blind man's eyes, and said to him, "Go wash in the pool of Siloe (which means 'sent')." So he went away and washed and returned seeing. The neighbors and those who were used to seeing him as a beggar began saying, "Isn't this the man who used to sit and beg?" Some said, "It's he." But others said, "No, he just looks like him." Yet the man declared, "I am he."

So they said to him, "How were your eyes opened?" He answered, "The man called Jesus made clay and anointed my eyes and said to me, 'Go to the pool of Siloe and wash.' And I went and washed, and I see." They said to him, "Where is He?" He said, "I don't know."

They took him to the Pharisees. Now it was a Sabbath on which Jesus made the clay and opened his eyes. So the Pharisees asked him again how he received his sight. He said to them, "He put clay on my eyes, and I washed, and I see."

Some of the Pharisees said of Jesus, "This man is not from God. He doesn't keep the Sabbath." But others said, "How can a man who is a sinner work these signs?" They were divided. So they said to the blind man again, "What do you say of the man who opened your eyes?" He said, "He's a prophet."

So the Jews did not believe him when he said he had been blind and had got his sight. They called his parents and questioned them. "Is this your son, of whom you say that he was born blind? How then does he now see?" His parents answered, "We know that this is our son and that he was born blind. But how he now sees we don't know, or who opened his eyes we don't know. Ask him. He's of age. Let him speak for himself." They said this because they were afraid of the Jews. The Jews had agreed that if anyone were to confess Jesus to be the Christ, he should be put out of the synagogue.

So the Jews called the man a second time and said to him, "Give glory to God! We know this man is a sinner." He said, "Whether He's a sinner I don't know. One thing I do know, that whereas I was blind, now I see." So they said to him, "What did He do to you? How did He open your eyes?" He answered them, "I have told you already, and you have heard. Why would you hear it again? Would you become His disciples too?" They sneered at him and said, "You're His disciple, but we're disciples of Moses. We know God spoke to Moses, but as for this man, we don't know where He comes from." The man answered, "Why, here's a marvel - you don't know where He comes from, and yet He opened my eyes. We know that God doesn't listen to sinners, but if anyone worships Him and does His will, him He hears. Not from the beginning of the world has it been heard that anyone opened the eyes of a man born blind. If this man were not from God He could do nothing." They answered, "You were altogether born in sin, and you're teaching us?" They turned him out.

Jesus heard that they had thrown him out, and when He had found him, He said to him, "Do you believe in the Son of God?" He answered, "Who is he, Lord, that I may believe in him?" Jesus said to him, "You have both seen Him, and He it is who is speaking with you." He said, "I believe, Lord." And he fell down and worshipped Him.

Jesus said, "For judgment have I come into this world, that those who do not see may see, and those who do see may become blind." Some of the pharisees who were with Him heard this, and they said to Him, "Are we blind too?"

Jesus said to them, "If you were blind, you would not have sin. But now that you say, 'We see,' your sin remains."

Jesus said, "I tell you the truth, the man who enters, not by the door of the sheepfold, but climbs up another way, is a thief and a robber. But the man who enters by the door is shepherd of the sheep. To this man the gatekeeper opens, and the sheep hear his voice, and he calls his own sheep by name and leads them out. When he has let out his own sheep, he goes before them, and the sheep follow him because they know his voice. But a stranger they won't follow, but will run away from him, because they don't know the voice of strangers."

"I tell you the truth, I am the door of the sheep. All that have come are thieves and robbers. But the sheep have not heard them. I am the door. If anyone enter by me he shall be safe, and shall go in and out, and shall find pastures. The thief comes only to steal and kill and destroy. I have come that they may have life, and have it more abundantly."

"I am the Good Shepherd. The Good Shepherd lays down His life for His sheep. But the hireling, who is not a shepherd, whose own the sheep are not, sees the wolf coming and leaves the sheep and runs away. And the wolf snatches and scatters the sheep."

"I am the Good Shepherd, and I know mine, and mine know me, even as the Father knows me and I know the Father. I lay down my life for my sheep. Other sheep I have that are not of this fold. Them also I must bring, and they shall hear my voice, and there shall be one fold and one Shepherd. For this reason the Father loves me, that I lay down my life that I may take it up again. No one takes it from me, but I lay it down of myself. I have the power to lay it down, and I have the power to take it up again. Such is the command I have received from my Father."

Because of these words a division again arose among the Jews. Many of them were saying, "He has a devil. He's mad. Why do you listen to Him?" Others said, "These are not the words of one who has a devil. Can a devil open the eyes of the blind?"

+

Jesus spent the next two months in or about Jerusalem. Perhaps He stayed at least some of the time at the home of Mary, Martha and Lazarus at Bethany. Bethany was not far from Jerusalem, located on the road from the city that first swings up over the Mount of Olives and then drops sharply down to Jericho. At any rate, He was at their house one day when Mary, seated at His feet, was listening to His words. Martha was getting the meal ready and came up and said, "Lord, is it no concern of yours that my sister has left me to serve alone? Tell her to help me." But Jesus answered, "Martha, Martha, you are anxious and troubled about many things. Yet only one thing is necessary. Mary has chosen the best part, and it is not going to be taken away from her."

Then it was winter, December. The feast of the Dedication of the Temple took place at Jerusalem. Jesus was walking there, in Solomon's porch. The Jews gathered around Him and said to Him, "How long are you going to keep us in suspense? If you're the Christ, tell us openly."

Jesus answered, "I tell you, and you don't believe. The things I do in the name of my Father bear witness to me. But you don't believe because you're not of my sheep. My sheep hear my voice, and I know them, and they follow me. And I give them eternal life. And they shall never be lost, nor shall anyone snatch them out of my hand. My Father is greater than all in what He has given me, and there is no snatching out of His hand. The Father and I are one."

Again they picked up stones to stone Him. Jesus said, "Many good deeds have I shown you from my Father. For which of these are you going to stone me?" They answered, "Not for any good deed, but for blasphemy, because you, who are only a man, call yourself God."

Jesus said, "Isn't it written in your Law, 'I said you are gods'? If it calls them gods to whom the word of God was addressed and the Scripture cannot be broken - do you say of Him whom the Father has made holy and sent into the world, 'You blaspheme,' because I said, 'I am the Son of God'? If I do not perform my Father's deeds, don't believe me. But if I do perform them, and you are not willing to believe me, believe the deeds, that you may know and believe that the Father is in me and I in the Father."

They tried to seize Him, but He went away out of their hands.

He went away beyond the Jordan to where John had baptized, and there He stayed. Many people came to Him. They were saying, "John didn't perform any signs. But everything John said about this Man is true."

+

Jesus received word that Lazarus, the brother of Mary and Martha of Bethany, was sick. He went to Bethany, and we all know the beautiful story of His tears and the love that raised Lazarus from the dead. This miracle or "sign" caused many of the Jews to believe in Jesus, but it caused some others to go away to the Pharisees and tell them what Jesus had done.

Then the chief priests and the Pharisees gathered together in council. They said, "What are we doing? This man is performing many signs. If we leave Him alone, everyone will believe in Him, and the Romans will come in and sweep away both our sanctuary and our nation." But one of them, Caiaphas, the high priest that year, said to them, "You know nothing at all. Nor do you reflect that it is expedient for us that one man die for the people, instead of the whole nation being lost."

St. John remarks that he didn't say this of himself, but being high priest that year, prophesied that Jesus was to die for the nation, "and not only for that nation, but to gather into one all the scattered children of God." From that day on their determination to put Jesus to death hardened into a plan.

So Jesus no longer went about openly, but withdrew to the district near the desert to a town called Ephraim, and there He stayed with His disciples.

Then it was spring once more, and the Feast of the Passover was near. Many people from the country went up to Jerusalem beforehand in order to purify themselves. They were looking for Jesus. As they stood in the Temple they were saying to one another, "What do you think? That He's not coming to the Feast?" The chief priests and Pharisees had given orders that if anyone knew where He was, he should report it, so that they might take Him.

At length the day finally came, and Jesus set out for

Jerusalem with His disciples for the last time. They were on their way, and Jesus was walking on in front of them. The disciples were in dismay. They were afraid. He began to tell the Twelve what would happen to Him. "We are going up to Jerusalem, and everything that has been written by the prophets about the Son of Man will be accomplished. He will be betrayed to the chief priests and the Scribes, and they will condemn Him to death and deliver Him to the Gentiles. They will mock Him and spit on Him and scourge Him, and after they have scourged Him, they will put Him to death, and on the third day He will rise again." The evangelist says they understood none of this.

He passed through Jericho, and "six days before the Passover" arrived at Bethany. There a supper was given for Him, where Mary Magdalen, the sister of Martha and Lazarus, anointed His head and feet with expensive perfume and wiped them dry with her hair. Judas saw it, complained that it was a waste of money that could have been given to the poor, and being rebuked by Jesus - "Let her alone! Let her keep it for my burial" - went off to the chief priests to hand Jesus over to them. They promised him money, and from that time on he was looking for an opportunity to hand Jesus over.

XII

Let Not Your Heart Be Troubled

The next day was the day we now call Passion or Palm Sunday. Jesus left Bethany for Jerusalem. We know the story of how, as he and His disciples came to Bethphage on the Mount of Olives, He sent two of them into the village ahead of them with instructions to get "the colt of an ass" on which He would ride triumphantly into Jerusalem. The procession that followed we re-enact every year Liturgically. The crowd was enthusiastic, because Jesus' raising of Lazarus was still fresh in its memory.

We know the story of how Jesus wept over Jerusalem. Then He entered the Temple, healed the blind and lame there, looked around at everything, and then left and went out to Bethany and spent the night there with His disciples.

Monday morning, on their way back to Jerusalem, Jesus cursed the fig tree that had nothing to provide for His hunger. It seems that in the Temple He once again purged it of all the commerce, and at evening left the city once more.

Returning Tuesday morning, He and the disciples all saw the fig tree "withered from the roots." Jesus told the amazed disciples, "All things whatsoever you ask for in prayer, believe that you shall receive, and it shall be done to you."

In the Temple He denounced the chief priests and elders, and concluded, "Jerusalem! Jerusalem! You who kill the prophets and stone the messengers sent to you! How often would I have gathered your children together as a hen gathers her young, but you would not!"

He praised the poor widow who put two small copper coins in the Temple Treasury, "all she had to live on."

He cried out, "Whoever believes in me believes, not in me, but in Him who sent me. And whoever sees me sees Him who sent me. I have come a Light into the world, that whoever believes in me may not remain in the darkness. If anyone hears my words and does not keep them, it is not I who will judge him, for I have not come to judge the world, but to save the world. Whoever rejects me and does not accept my words already has his judge. The word that I have spoken will condemn him on the last day."

He left the Temple and spent the night teaching the disciples on the Mount of Olives. He now spent the days teaching in the Temple and the nights on Mount Olivet.

The next day, Wednesday, the chief priests and elders gathered together in the court of the high priest, Caiaphas, and plotted how to take Jesus by stealth and put Him to death. "Not on the Feast," they said, "or there might be a riot." They were afraid of the people.

Then, on the evening of "the first day of Unleavened Bread," Thursday, when it was customary for them to sacrifice the Passover, Jesus reclined at table with the Twelve. He said to them, "I have greatly desired to eat this Passover with you before I suffer. I tell you, I will not eat it again until it has been fulfilled in the Kingdom of God."

After a little while a dispute began to arise among the

Twelve as to which of them was the greatest. Jesus said to them, "The kings of the nations lord it over them....It is not to be so with you. On the contrary, let him who is the greatest among you be as the youngest, and him who is the leader as the servant. For which is the greater, he who reclines at table, or he who serves? Is it not he who reclines? But I am among you as the One who serves you...."

Then, says St. John, "Knowing that His hour had come to pass out of this world to the Father, Jesus, having loved His own who were in the world, loved them to the end." He continues, "Jesus, knowing that the Father had put everything in His hands, and that He had come from God and was going to God, rose from the supper and took off His cloak and took a towel and tied it around Himself. Then He poured water into a basin and began to wash the feet of the disciples, drying them with the towel."

We know the story of Peter's resistance and then superabundant capitulation. After Jesus had washed their feet and put His cloak back on, when He had reclined again, He said to them, "Do you know what I have done to you? You call me Master and Lord, and rightly so, for that is what I am. If, then, I the Lord and Master have washed your feet, you also ought to wash the feet of one another."

St. John goes on, then "He began to be troubled in spirit and said solemnly, 'I tell you the truth, one of you will betray me.'" We know the story of their questions, their puzzlement, and Peter's beckoning to John to ask Jesus whom He meant. Jesus answered John, "It is he for whom I shall dip the bread and give it to him." He dipped a morsel of bread and gave it to Judas. St. John says, "After the morsel, Satan entered into him. Then Judas, who betrayed Him, answered, 'Is it I, Rabbi?' He said to him, 'You have said it.' Jesus said to him, 'What you do, do quickly.'" When he had received the morsel, he went out quickly. St. John says, "It was night."

Jesus took bread, gave thanks and blessed and broke it and gave it to them and said, "Take and eat - this is my Body, which will be given up for you." Later He took a cup of wine, gave thanks and gave it to them and said, "All of you drink of this, for this is my Blood of the New Covenant, which will be shed for you and for many for the forgiveness of sins." He told them, "Do this in memory of me," and gave them a "new commandment" - "Love one another as I have loved you."

Jesus spoke of going where they could not follow. We know the story of Peter's asking why he could not follow, since he was ready to go even to death with Him, and how Jesus foretold Peter's three denials.

Then He continued speaking to them. "Let not your heart be troubled. You believe in God. Believe likewise in me." He told them He was going to prepare a place for them, that He would return to take them to be with Him forever. He said He would send them another Helper, the Spirit of Truth, to be with them permanently and to take His place as their Teacher. He spoke of how, because of the Holy Spirit, He and His Father would come to them and make Their abode in them. "Peace I leave you," He said, "my peace...." He spoke of Himself as the True Vine in which they must continue to abide in order to bear fruit. And He spoke of how He was going to lay down His life for them, for love of them. He told them they would be hated and persecuted, just as He was, but in the end their suffering would be turned into joy. He told them to ask, that this joy of theirs might be complete.

Then after speaking thus for a long time, He raised His eyes to Heaven and prayed, "Father, the hour has come. Glorify Your Son, that Your Son may give glory to You...." He prayed for the Twelve, for their unity. He prayed for their joy, and that His Father would keep them from evil. "Sanctify them...." He prayed also for all who through their word would come to believe. He prayed for the final unity of all these in Him and in His Father. In His prayer He gathered up the sum total of all these precious souls, a world, a universe of human hearts, and said, "Father, I will that where I am they also whom You have given me may be with me, to behold my glory, which You have given me, because You have loved me, before the creation of the world." He continued, "Just Father, the world has not known You, but I have known You, and these men have known that You have sent me. And I have made known to them Your name, and will make it known, that the love with which you have loved me may be in them, and I in them."

It was late now. They all got up and left the house and went out across the Kidron Valley, as He had been doing for several days, to the Mount of Olives. They came to a place called Gethsemane, where there was a garden, which He and His disciples entered. He said to them, "Sit down here while I go over yonder and pray. Pray that you may not be subjected to trial."

He took with Him Peter and James and John. Then it was that He began to be afraid and to be filled with distress. He said to them, "My soul is in anguish, even to the point of death. Stay here and keep awake." He withdrew from them about a stone's throw. He knelt down, fell on the ground, and began to pray that, if it were possible, the hour might pass Him by. He prayed, "Father, everything is possible for You. If You are willing, remove this cup from me. Yet not as I will, but as You will."

Then He came back to them and found them sleeping. He said to Peter, "Simon, are you asleep? Couldn't you stay awake one hour with me? Keep awake and pray, that you may not be subjected to trial. The spirit is willing, but the flesh is weak."

Again a second time He went away and prayed. "My Father, if this cup cannot pass away unless I drink it, Your will be done." He came to them again and found them sleeping. Their eyes were heavy. They didn't know what answer to make to Him.

He left them and went back again and prayed a third time, in the same words. An angel appeared to Him from Heaven to strengthen Him. He fell into an agony and prayed the more earnestly. His sweat became drops of blood running down onto the ground.

He got up from His prayer and came to the disciples and found them sleeping, exhausted with grief. He said to them, "Still sleeping? Still taking your rest? Why do you sleep? Get up and pray, that you may not be subjected to trial."

"It will have to do. The hour has come. Look, the Son of Man is betrayed into the hands of sinners."

As he spoke, Judas, who knew the place well since Jesus had often met there with His disciples, appeared with the cohort as well as guards supplied by the chief priests and the Pharisees, with lanterns and torches and weapons, a big crowd with swords and clubs. Judas had given them a sign. "Whomever I kiss is the one. Take Him and lead Him securely away." He came straight up to Jesus and said, "Rabbi!" and kissed Him. Jesus said to him, "Friend, why have you come? Judas, do you betray the Son of Man with a kiss?"

Knowing all that was about to happen to Him, Jesus stepped forward and said to the crowd, "Whom do you seek?" They answered Him, "Jesus of Nazareth." Jesus said to them, "I am He." When He said this, Judas and the others all fell backward to the ground.

So He asked them again, "Whom do you seek?" They said, "Jesus of Nazareth." Jesus answered, "I have told you that I am He. If, then, you want me, let these others go their way" - that the word might be fulfilled, "Of those whom You have given me I have not lost one." Then they came forward and laid hands on Jesus and took Him.

But when the disciples saw what was happening, they said to Him, "Lord, shall we strike with the sword?" Simon Peter had a sword and drew it and struck the servant of the high priest and cut off his right ear. The servant's name was Malchus. Jesus answered, "Enough!" - and He touched his ear and healed him. Jesus said to Peter, "Put up your sword into the scabbard. All those who take up the sword will perish by the sword. Or do you suppose that I cannot ask my Father, and He will even now furnish me with more than twelve legions of angels? Shall I not drink the cup that the Father has given me? Otherwise, how would the Scriptures be fulfilled, that it must happen like this?"

Then He said to the crowd - the chief priests, the leaders of the Temple guard, and the elders - who had come against Him, "As against a robber you have come out, with swords and clubs. I sat daily with you in the Temple teaching, and you did not lay hands on me. But this is your hour and the power of darkness." The evangelist says that all this took place that the writings of the prophets might be fulfilled.

Then the soldiers of the cohort and the tribune and the Jewish guards took Jesus and bound Him. At this, says the evangelist, "all His disciples abandoned Him and fled."

+

It is all very troubling - the whole story of Judas' betrayal, and then Peter's protestations of utter loyalty, which in the light of his subsequent denials fill us with fear.

It is precisely because of these things, and because He knew that "in the world" we would "have distress," that Jesus went on, "Let not your heart be troubled." He would speak long of His love for us all, and of the power of the Holy Spirit of Truth to confirm us in fidelity and peace.

He was going to prepare a place for us. He was going to accomplish a sacrificial death that would win for us the grace to reach that Heavenly place prepared for each of us from all Eternity.

He said that He would come again - meaning either at our individual deaths or at the end of the world - to take us to Himself, that where He is we also may be.

He spoke of how the Father and He would come and live in our hearts, and how the Holy Spirit too would dwell within us as in His temples, and how this Divine Indwelling would bless us and prepare us for Paradise.

He spoke of how He is the True Vine and His Father is the Vinegrower, of how we must "abide" in Him in order to bear spiritual fruit, and of how the more spiritually fruitful we are, the more the Father will trim us clean, that we may become even more fruitful.

He gave us the answer to the problem of suffering. "In this is my Father glorified, that you bear very much fruit." For it is only in becoming truly fruitful in the Holy Spirit through much suffering that we really become Christ's disciples.

It hurts. Growing so much hurts very much. But we know that as the Father loves Jesus, even that much does Jesus love us.

He tells us to "abide" in His love - by keeping His commandments, just as He has obeyed the Father and "abides" in the Father's love. He speaks to us that our joy may be complete - for the commandment is that we love one another.

We are to love as He loves. We are to lay down our lives for one another, just as He laid down His for us all. This will make us, no longer merely His servants, but true friends, who follow the way of free and noble love even as He did for our sakes.

Our strength will be in His promise that whatever we ask the Father in His name He will do for us.

The world will hate us, but it hated Him first. The world will persecute us, just as it persecuted Him who is our Master and has gone before us.

It is because we are not of the world, but He has chosen us out of the world, that the world hates us.

The hour is coming for everyone who kills us to think he is offering worship to God – because such people do not know God, neither the Father nor Jesus.

The Spirit of Truth will come, sent from the Father and from Jesus, to fill us all with the strength of the truth.

We shall weep and lament, while the world rejoices. We will be sorrowful, but our sorrow will be transformed into joy, just as a woman about to give birth suffers pangs, but afterwards no longer remembers them for her joy that a child has been born into the world.

We have sorrow in this world of time, but some day we will see "this Jesus" once again, and our hearts will rejoice, and our joy no one will ever be able to take away from us.

But even in this world we will have joy, if only we are faithful to lives of prayer. He urges us all passionately, "Ask! That your joy may be complete!" And He assures us emphatically, "I do not say that I will ask the Father for you, for the Father Himself loves you, because you have loved me, and have believed that I came forth from Him."

He assures us that He knows our frame, that even in our cowardly weakness He will be with us, to get us through all trials to victory in the end. He speaks to us that in Him we may have peace. In the world we will always have distress. But He is our Confidence and our Courage, for He has overcome the world.

Then Jesus prayed. He prayed to the Father, beseeching Him to glorify Him with the glory He had with Him before the world existed, that He Himself in turn might glorify the Father by giving eternal life to all of us sheep whom the Father has entrusted to His care.

Jesus has taught us the truth, and we have believed in

Him. We know that He came forth from the Father, was sent by the Father.

He prays that our faith may not fail. He prays for us because the Father has given us to Him, and we therefore belong to Him, and He loves us. He prays that we may all be one, even as the Father and He are one, in the wonderful Holy Spirit of Truth.

Jesus has spoken to us that we may have His joy complete in our own hearts. He prays to the Father to sanctify us in truth, to make us truly holy. He re-consecrates Himself to the Father for our sakes, that we too may be consecrated in Him who is our Truth.

He prays for all who are to believe in Him, "that all may be one," Jesus in us and the Father in Jesus, that the total unity of all may be complete, that the world may see and know that it really was the Father who sent Jesus, and that the Father loves us all even as He loves Jesus.

Then his prayer becomes a positive demand of love. "Father, I will that where I am they also whom You have given me may be with me, that they may see my glory, which You have given me, because You have loved me, before the creation of the world." He wills that we His brothers and sisters may be with Him in Beatifying Vision of His own Divinity.

He concludes, "Just Father, the world has not known You, but I have known You, and these have known that You have sent me. I have made known Your name to them, and will continue to make it known, in order that the love with which You have loved me may be in them, and I in them."

Jesus has taught us all to call God our Father, for such He truly is. We are to speak to the Father in humility and confidence, that the Holy Spirit and Jesus Himself may live in our hearts by means of His own unique, true, deep and lasting peace.

He had told the Apostles, "I will ask the Father, and He will send you another Advocate, the Spirit of Truth, to be with you forever." Jesus Himself has been our Advocate from the beginning, praying always that our faith might not fail, and now in Heaven living on even there to continue to intercede for us. But now that Pentecost has come, He has sent us another Advocate, One who prays for us even from within our own hearts and confirms us in the realization that we are God's children.

The Eucharist, service, unity, suffering - these are themes that all go together. And they are all summed up in the "Paraclete," the Gift of God, the Holy Spirit whom Jesus would send from the Father, and whom the Father Himself would send at Jesus' prayer, "that all may be one."

To bring it about Jesus would suffer. To continue His work we too must suffer. But He said, "Let not your heart be troubled...." We have need of these words, just as we have need of Him. His Presence in the Eucharist, Holy Thursday's Gift to us - the Sacrament of Victory - strengthens us to suffer as He did for unity. It fills us with confidence and energy - He Himself remaining among us in the Mystery of Faith.

There is much to suffer - sometimes we pray with Him, "Father, if it be possible...." - and yet He continues to say to us, "Let not your heart be troubled." We have the victory in "our faith." We have only to "live it out."

Jesus suffered, and for the time being, he suffered alone. He says to all of us, "Let not your heart be troubled." But in the Garden of Gethsemane His own Heart was very much troubled. It was by prayer that He won the victory over that terrible anguish and was able manfully to proceed.

He proceeded alone. He was bound and taken away. The disciples were scattered and terrified. It was reality, and reality was terrible. Words, protestations had come easy, and reality had scattered them all to the winds.

Yet Jesus Himself was the Most Real Reality, the Reality of God in our world. He was doing what He had come into this world to do. He was doing it in a manly way.

He was the Great Shepherd of the Sheep. He was God. He was doing for the sheep what they could not do for themselves. He was fighting the wolf. The wolf would wreak havoc with His physical body, but the sheep would be saved.

And the Great Shepherd would slay the wolf. Physically it would cost Him a lot, the crucifixion of His physical body. But in His Divinity He would triumph over death, and He would feed His beloved sheep with His slain and risen Body and his Precious Blood.

He knew beforehand all that was going to happen. All the terrible evil of it was only part of a superior Divine Plan that transcended the weakness of human freedom. It was the Perfect Plan of an Almighty God. It was the Plan of an all wise God that was going to work. It was the Plan of an all good, suffering God - *Deus Patiens* - who would make it work by the power of His love.

It was an Eternal Plan, to deliver the sheep from death and "preserve them in spite of famine." It was the Eucharistic Plan of God's Heart. Nothing could thwart it. At the last moment, when all seemed lost, He would triumph even in death, but not before He had revealed His final secret, that in the awful famine of this world He Himself would become the Food of His poor sheep.

He has been delivered up, and now it is the end. He is on His way to death. But this was why He was born and why He came into the world, to teach us all the way of truth, to be a Leader.

As he moves forward he is blazing a trail, a trail we could never even have found, much less followed, without Him. He has scattered it with graces of strength and fidelity. He has left footsteps for us to follow in.

His courage will be our confidence.

We too have to follow a Way of the Cross, but not in the darkness - rather in the splendid light of Him who has marked it out for us. Keeping "our eyes fixed on **Jesus**," we will be able to do it, even we poor, dumb, stupid sheep - even we sinners. We will be made strong in the contemplation of Him who has loved us. His Victory will be the pledge of ours, and in a very real sense, will be ours.

He is going to suffer. He has suffered agony in the Garden. There will be more agony, greater agony. But in the end there will be the Victory of Life and Peace.

For us too there will be suffering. But there will be for us the grace of knowing that the Great Shepherd of our souls, who waits ahead for us, has made the whole Way of the Cross a way of love. He has given us the victory of love and peace in "our faith."

That One Man Die for the People

We know the story. Jesus was brought to Annas. Annas sent Him on, still bound, to his son-in-law, Caiaphas. "Caiaphas was the one who had given the counsel that it was expedient that one man should die for the people."

Midnight came, and the "trial" dragged on. Peter's denials, Jesus' condemnation, Judas' remorse - all followed one another in the chilly darkness.

At daybreak the whole Sanhedrin and all the assembly led Jesus away to the praetorium and Pontius Pilate, the Governor. Another "trial" would go on and on.

Pilate could see that Jesus was innocent. His innocence made him nervous. "What is truth?... Have you no answer to make to them?" Pilate grasped at a straw. He heard Galilee mentioned and tried sending Jesus to Herod, the ruler of Galilee, but Herod sent Him back, unable to get anything out of Him.

Pilate was afraid. He kept trying. He tried Barabbas. The crowd wouldn't have it. Pilate's wife sent him the message about her dream.

The crowd demanded, "Crucify Him!" Pilate said, "Why? What evil has He done? I find no crime deserving of death in Him. I'm going to whip Him and release Him." The logic of cowardice.

But the crowd kept crying, "Crucify Him! Crucify Him!"

And their cries prevailed.

But first Pilate took Jesus and had Him whipped. The soldiers called together the whole cohort, stripped Jesus and whipped Him. Then they put a purple cloak over Him, fashioned a kind of helmet of thorns as a crown, put a reed in His right hand, and then came up and genuflected before Him, mocking Him, "Hail! King of the Jews!" They spat on Him and hit Him on the head with the reed.

Pilate brought Jesus out wearing the crown of thorns and the purple cloak and said to the crowd, "Look at the Man!"

It didn't work. They kept crying, "Crucify Him! Crucify Him!"

He took Jesus back into the praetorium and said to Him, "Where are You from?" Jesus gave him no answer. Pilate said to Him, "You're not speaking to me? Don't You know I have power to crucify You and to release You?" Jesus answered, "You would have no power over me at all were it not given you from Above. Therefore the man who betrayed me to you has the greater sin."

Pilate made one last try. He took Jesus outside again and said to the Jews, "Look at your King!" They answered, "We have no king but Caesar!" Then Pilate took water and washed his hands in the sight of the crowd and said, "I am innocent of the blood of this just man. See to it yourselves." All the people answered, "His blood be on us and on our children."

Then Pilate handed Jesus over to them to be crucified. They mocked Him, took the cloak off Him and put His own clothes back on Him, and led Him away to crucify Him.

Bearing the Cross Himself, He went out to the place called the Skull, in Hebrew, "Golgotha."

As he went along He became weaker and weaker. Finally, the procession encountered a man from Cyrene named Simon, known later in the early Church as "the father of Alexander and Rufus," who was coming in from the country. He was forced to take up the Cross and carry it along after Jesus.

A great crowd of people was following Jesus, including a large number of women, who were weeping and lamenting for Him. He turned to them and said, "Daughters of Jerusalem, don't weep for me, weep for yourselves and for your children. For the days are coming when men will be saying, 'Blessed are the barren, the wombs that never bore, the breasts that never nursed.' Then they will begin saying to the mountains, 'Fall on us,' and to the hills, 'Cover us,' for if they are doing these things to the green wood, what will happen in the case of the dry?"

Tradition says He encountered His Mother, Mary, somewhere along the way. But we cannot begin to describe the terrible anguish of that meeting, the terrible anguished love.

He came to the place called Golgotha. Then they crucified Him there. They gave Him some wine to drink mixed with gall, but when He had tasted it, He refused to drink it. They crucified two robbers with Him, one on His right and one on His left. Jesus was in the center. The Scripture was fulfilled which says, "And he was reckoned among the wicked."

Pilate had written an inscription and had it put on the Cross - "Jesus of Nazareth, the King of the Jews." Many of the Jews read this inscription, because the place where Jesus was crucified was near the city, and it was written in Hebrew, in Greek and in Latin. So the chief priests of the Jews went to Pilate and said to him, "Don't write, 'The King of the Jews,' but, 'He said, I am the King of the Jews.'" Pilate answered, "What I have written, I have written."

Jesus was lifted up on the Cross. Suddenly He spoke, in prayer: "Father, forgive them. They don't know what they're doing."

The soldiers had divided His clothes into four parts, to each soldier a part. But there was also the tunic. Now the tunic was without seam, woven in one piece from the top by Jesus' Mother. So they said to one another, "Let's not tear it. Let's throw dice to see who gets it" - that the Scripture might be fulfilled which says, "They divided my garments among them, for my clothing they cast lots." Then the soldiers sat down to keep watch over Him.

The people stood looking on. The passers-by insulted Him. They would say, "You who destroy the Temple and rebuild it in three days, save yourself! If you're the Son of God, come down from that Cross!" Similarly, the chief priests with the Scribes and the elders mocked Him and said, "He saved others, Himself he can't save! If he's the King of Israel, let him come down now from the cross, and we'll believe him. Let him save himself if he's the Christ, the chosen one of God. He trusted in God, let God deliver him now if He loves him - since he said, 'I am the Son of

God.'"

The soldiers mocked Him too, coming up to Him and offering Him their sour wine and saying, "If you're the King of the Jews, save yourself!"

The robbers too, who were crucified with Him, taunted Him in the same way. At least one of them did. He was saying, "If you're the Christ, save yourself and us!" But the other rebuked him and said, "Don't you even fear God, seeing that you're under the same sentence? And we indeed justly. We're getting what our deeds deserved. But this man has done nothing wrong." Then he said to Jesus, "Lord, remember me when You come into Your Kingdom." Jesus said to him, "I tell you the truth, this day you will be with me in paradise."

His Mother was standing by the Cross, with John the Apostle and with her relative, Mary of Cleophas, and Mary Magdalen. When Jesus saw His Mother standing there and the disciple whom He loved, He said to His Mother, "Woman, there is your son." Then He said to the disciple, "Son, there is your Mother." From that moment the disciple took her as his own.

From noon until about three in the afternoon there was darkness over the whole land. Then Jesus cried out loudly in Hebrew, "My God, my God, why have You abandoned me?" When they heard this, some of the bystanders said, "Look, he's calling on Elijah."

After this, knowing that everything was now accomplished, that the Scripture might be fulfilled, Jesus said, "I thirst." There was a container full of cheap wine there. Immediately one of the bystanders ran and took a sponge and soaked it in the wine, put it on the end of a reed, and offered it to Him to drink. He said, "Now let's see whether Elijah comes to take him down." When Jesus had taken the wine, He said, "It is consummated," and then cried out loudly, "Father, into Your hands I commend my spirit." When He had said this, He breathed His last.

Then the curtain of the Temple in the city was torn in two from top to bottom, there was an earthquake, boulders split, tombs opened. Many bodies of saints who had fallen asleep arose. After His Resurrection they came out of the tombs and came into the holy city and appeared to many people.

When the centurion standing at the Cross saw what had happened, he glorified God and said, "This really was a just man. He really was the Son of God." The soldiers with him keeping guard over Jesus and all the crowd that had gathered for the sight, when they saw the earthquake and the things that were happening, were very much afraid. They said, "He really was the Son of God," and they began to return to the city, beating their breasts.

All His friends, and the women who had followed Him from Galilee, were standing at a distance looking on. There were many women. Mary Magdalen was among them, and Mary, the mother of James and Joseph, and the mother of the sons of Zebedee.

It was Preparation Day. So in order that the bodies might not remain on the Cross on the Sabbath (for that Sabbath was a solemn day), the Jews asked Pilate that their legs might be broken and that they might be taken away. So the soldiers came up and broke the legs of the two who had been crucified with Jesus, but when they came to Jesus, and saw that He was already dead, they didn't break His legs.

But one of the soldiers opened His side with a lance, and immediately blood and water came out. St. John remarks that these things happened that the Scripture might be fulfilled, "Not a bone of him shall you break," and "They shall look on him whom they have pierced."

When it was evening, a certain rich man of Arimathea came along, Joseph by name, a good and just man, a councillor of high rank, who likewise was looking for the Kingdom of God. He had not been party to their plan of action. He was a disciple of Jesus, although for fear of the Jews a secret one. He asked Pilate to let him take away the body of Jesus.

Pilate was surprised that Jesus should have died so soon. He sent for the centurion and asked him if Jesus was already dead. When he learned from the centurion that he was, he granted the body to Joseph.

Nicodemus also came, who had come to Jesus at first by night. He brought a mixture of myrrh and aloes, weighing about a hundred pounds. So they took the body of Jesus and wrapped it in linen cloths with the perfumed oils, after the Jewish manner of preparing for burial.

Now in the place where Jesus was crucified there was a garden, and in the garden there was a new tomb which Joseph had hewn out of the rock, in which no one had yet been laid. So because it was Preparation Day, and the tomb was close at hand, they laid Jesus there. Joseph rolled a great stone to the entrance of the tomb and then left.

Mary Magdalen and Mary, the mother of James and Joseph, had followed after and seen the tomb and how His body was laid. They went back and prepared spices and ointments. They rested during the Sabbath, according to the commandment.

Meanwhile, the chief priests and Pharisees had gone in a body to Pilate and said, "Sir, we remember how that deceiver said while he was still alive, 'After three days I will rise again.' Give orders, then, that the tomb be guarded until the third day, or else his disciples may come and steal him away and say to the people, 'He has risen from the dead,' and the last imposture will be worse than the first."

Pilate said to them, "You have a guard. Go guard it as well as you know how." So they went and made the tomb secure, sealing the stone and setting up a guard.

+

Do we see ourselves in Pilate - desiring the good, desiring to be true, yet not really knowing even what truth is? "The agreement of the mind with reality." And is reality this kind of expedience?

We are weak. We are cowards. We are very much like Pilate. We struggle feebly for the good. We want to be true. But the cries of the majority prevail - and we give in, or at least we compromise.

We don't want to. It makes us sick. But we just don't have the strength to do anything else. We are not heroes.

No, we are not true.

And yet there is something in us that is "of the truth." We hear the voice of Jesus Christ. "Everyone who is of the truth hears my voice."

We hear Him promising that He will always be with us.

Of ourselves we are no better than Pilate. Yet we believe in Jesus Christ. He has given us all the grace and gift of trust in Himself. He has promised final victory to all who rely on Him absolutely and trust in His power to save.

We are pitiful. Yet we cling to this hope.

The only good things about us are that we know our weakness and we pray. But often we are unfaithful even to prayer. When you get right down to it, the only really good thing about us is His grace in our souls, which makes us members of Himself.

"No one is good except God alone." We contemplate Pilate, and ourselves, and we realize that it is the absolute truth.

And yet there is for us "the Spirit of grace and prayers." We remember Jesus' words, "If you, evil as you are, know how to give good gifts to your children, how much more will your Heavenly Father give His Good Spirit to those who ask Him." His Holy Spirit.

So we go on in the way of prayer, struggling against our own cowardly falsehood, struggling to be - or to become - true.

It is a gift of grace - we know it. It is humility.

"Learn of me, for I am meek and humble of heart." We see it in His trials before Caiaphas and Herod and Pilate more than anywhere else. When struck in the face, He quietly answers, "If I said something wrong, show us what was wrong in it. If not, why do you hit me?" And when it gets to the point where we would rage insanely, He simply is silent. *Jesus autem tacebat.*

"Humility, humility, humility," said St. Augustine. It is the answer of all the saints.

+

It was "the Passion of Our Lord Jesus Christ," the *Via Dolorosa*, the Way of the Cross, crucifixion and finally death.

Let us walk with Him along the way, in an old fashioned meditation.

He had sweat blood in His agony in the Garden of Olives. He had been bound, and then blindfolded and slapped and struck and spat on, then crowned with thorns, whipped nearly to death, and mocked again. Physically, emotionally, mentally, He was exhausted. His whole body and soul ached with pain and suffering.

Then He was given the Cross to carry. Some say it was a single beam laid across His shoulders, to be fixed to an upright at the place of crucifixion. However this may be, the Greek of the Gospel says that what he carried was a "cross."

And indeed, it was so heavy for Him that He couldn't carry it all the way. Tradition says He fell - more than once. It seems quite likely. A passerby, Simon of Cyrene, was made to carry the Cross along behind Jesus.

They walked a gauntlet of hatred and abuse. Crowds can be extremely ugly. In crowds often no one understands anything. Passion is king. People go wild, finding evil satisfaction in punishing the defenseless and innocent simply for being that, sometimes in the name of "justice," but sometimes blatantly even in the devil's name.

This was such a crowd, kept at fever pitch by the religious leaders.

At length the procession arrives at the "Skull Place," the hill called Calvary outside the city, where criminals were executed.

Jesus was roughly forced down on the crossbeams, after being stripped, and then was nailed to them hands and feet with some kind of spikes.

He was raised up, and the Cross was roughly dropped into the hole dug for it. Every moment was an infinity of pain for Jesus Christ.

He was our God, and He was satisfying for our sins, to save us from hell, and to make us happy with Him in Heaven forever.

Then the soldiers settled down to wait. They laughed at Him. "He saved others. Himself He can't save."

Jesus hung there. Mary His Mother, and John and Mary Magdalen drew near.

We say it all so simply - and it was horror.

It lasted three hours - an eternity of anguish.

It was a cold and hateful world rejecting truth and love. It had gone on for centuries, and it continues even to this day.

The world says that anybody who doesn't have sense enough to take care of himself deserves to suffer.

If you're foolish enough to speak the truth when it's not "discreet," you'll have to take what you get.

The world has no sympathy for the Crucified. "I looked for sympathy, and there was none, for comforters, and I found none."

Except for Mary, His Mother - and with her, John and Mary Magdalen and, it seems, a few other women.

If we cannot imagine the sufferings of a God-Man, we can do little better in trying to enter into the anguish of Mary, His Virgin Mother, Co-Redemptrix and Mediatrix of All the Graces Jesus was winning for this world that was insulting His love and mercy.

Mary stood there. The Church says she did not waver. It seems she said not a word. Tradition says she wept, and it seems, silently.

The end came, and the soldier drove his lance into Christ's side, to make sure it was the end. He drove that lance into Mary's Heart, into her soul. At that moment, she "died without dying" - Queen and Mother of all martyrs.

Jesus Christ, "the Redeemer of man," supported and accompanied in a subordinate way by Mary, His Perfect and Perpetual Virgin Mother, had accomplished the task He came into this world to do. In dying He had destroyed death and all "the works of the devil."

The "darkness over all the land," and the curtain of the Temple - ripped mysteriously in two from top to bottom - and the earthquake, all proclaimed the Deicide that in God's Plan was Christ's Sacrifice of Himself in reparation for all the sins of the race He had come to bear back to the Father on His own shoulders.

He was the Good Shepherd, and He had ransomed the sheep. The wolf was dead, and Jesus Himself would return to new and gloriously unending Life on the third day.

"O Death, I will be your Death." The God-Man had led the way. A multitude of saints would follow - through darkness and death to the Light of True and Eternal Life.

+

The Centurion looked up at Jesus hanging dead on the Cross. Amidst all the weird natural phenomena, he was enabled to see. He said in awe, "This really was a just

Man. He really was the Son of God." And the whole crowd left the scene, the Gospel says, "beating their breasts."

It's always like that with God and man. Man has the power to do terrible evil, but not to right the wrong. Only God can create goodness. When a free will chooses evil, only God can repair the damage.

But the goodness of God is as great as His power, and His power - as well as His wisdom - is infinite.

God believes in love. He believes in freedom. He has the answer - in His gift of grace. The answer lies in His infinite love for His poor creatures, His poor children.

The glory of God is the ultimate end, the ultimate goal, of creation and the Incarnation and our Redemption and Sanctification. But God glorifies Himself by granting the gift of happiness to His little children.

It is a sheer gift. No matter how deeply we may enter into the Redemptive suffering of Jesus - and of His sinless Mother, Mary - as the Council of Trent said so wonderfully, God makes His gifts to be our merits.

If we love, we will enter as deeply as possible into this meriting and this suffering. And it will be a sign. It will purify our hearts and bring us to truth and peace.

"Love is not loved!" cried Blessed Angela of Foligno.

All the saints have lived in the pure desire and heroic effort to respond to the Divine Love of Jesus Christ for us.

It is not hopeless. Once again, the secret is humility. Our love for Him consists principally in opening our own hearts wide to let in the torrents of His for us. Heroism is a gift that flows from Love. It's not the other way around. It is only Love, Love Personified, the Holy Spirit of Love, who makes the heroes and heroines of God. Only this

Divine Love is powerful enough.

We are little children. Love is our only strength, our only heroism.

We approach the crucifix as powerless little one's, who have nothing to give but our heart, together with its love. And this is all God wants. He doesn't need anything else. He possesses untold infinities of power and strength. The Human Heart of Jesus has no need but love.

Most Sacred Heart of Jesus, we place our trust in You.

O Lord our God, we trust in You to make us what we cannot make ourselves, perfect lovers, saints, martyrs, if it be Your will to grant us this last gift.

We have followed You this far, and we know that death is not the end.

We know that Your death was the beginning of Life for the whole sinful world. We believe in the Way of the Cross, because You have made it a way of Life and Love for us all.

Therefore we will keep going. It is all we have to do. To advance is to grow. To move forward along the way of suffering is to grow in love.

And You have made it for us a way of peace. There may be moments for us, when we cry out, "My God, my God, why....?" Yet because You have endured it to the utter depths, for us too they pass, and we find peace and quiet calmness once again.

Yes, You have made it for us a way of peace - not of continual, perfect peace, but nevertheless a true and real way of genuine and blessed peace.

We want to love, and You say to us simply, "Peace!"

Our desire is our love. Our obedience is our love.

Our peace is love - purified and perfected.

Like Mary Magdalen and the other women, we will obey - and wait. The passage of time will accomplish everything. In silence our hearts are being healed.

"Christ has died...." But You will rise again, O Lord our God.

And we will rise.

Holy Saturday is a day of waiting. *O Mors, ero Mors tua.* In fact, death is already dead.

We are waiting for the Victory of Life. We are waiting quietly for God, for the glorious manifestation of the Triumph of Jesus Christ.

"Wait for the Lord with courage. Be stouthearted, and wait for the Lord."

We are waiting with Mary, His Mother and ours, quietly - and there is peace.

It is a kind of peace of death, but of a death that has been conquered and transformed into pure and tranquil silence.

We are waiting in hope.

Like Mary, His Mother, we know in whom we have believed.

XIV

He Is Risen – He Is Not Here

The women waited till the Sabbath was over. Then, very early in the morning, just after sunrise, on "the first day of the week," our Sunday, they arrived at the tomb with perfumed oils with which they were going to anoint Jesus.

Meanwhile, at the tomb there had been a tremendous earthquake. An angel had come down and rolled back the stone and sat on it, his face like lightning and his clothing like snow. The guards had been terrified of him and had become like dead men.

When the women reached the tomb they saw that the large stone had been rolled back. They entered the tomb but "did not find the body of the Lord Jesus." Immediately Mary Magdalen ran off to Simon Peter "and the other disciple, the one Jesus loved," and told them, "The Lord has been taken from the tomb! We don't know where they have put Him!"

The women still at the tomb were wondering what to make of everything when suddenly two men stood by them dressed in dazzling clothes. The women were struck with fear and bowed low before them. One of the men said to them, "Don't be terrified. I know that you are looking for

Jesus, who was crucified. But why do you seek the Living One among the dead? He is not here, He has risen. Remember how He spoke to you while He was still in Galilee, and said that the Son of Man must be betrayed into the hands of sinful men, and be crucified, and on the third day rise again. Come see the place where the Lord was laid."

Then he continued, "Go quickly now, and tell His disciples that He has risen. He is going ahead of you into Galilee. There you will see Him as He told you." The women remembered Jesus' words and left the tomb, running away in fear and great joy.

It was true. Jesus Christ had risen from the dead. First of all He had appeared to Mary, His Mother. But about this mystery the Gospels are silent, and we shall be too.

Meanwhile, though, Peter and John had run off to the tomb. John outran Peter and reached the tomb first. He stooped down and saw the linen cloths lying there, but he didn't enter. Then Simon Peter came up and went into the tomb and saw the wrappings lying there, and the cloth which had covered Jesus' head, not lying with the wrappings, but folded up in a place by itself. Then John went in. He tells us himself, "He saw and believed." For as yet they had not understood the Scripture that Jesus must rise from the dead.

They went away wondering at it all.

Mary Magdalen had followed Peter and John back and stood outside the tomb weeping after they had gone away. Then, as she wept, she stooped and looked down into the tomb and saw two angels in white, sitting one at the head and one at the feet, where the body of the Lord Jesus had lain. They said to her, "Woman, why are you weeping?" She answered, "Because they have taken away my Lord, and I don't know where they have laid Him."

After she said this, she turned around and saw Jesus standing there, but she didn't know it was Jesus. He said to her, "Woman, why are you weeping?" She thought He was the gardener and said to Him, "Sir, if you have removed Him, tell me where you have laid Him, and I will take Him away." Jesus said to her, "Mary!" She turned full face to Him and said, "Rabboni!" - that is, "Master!" Jesus said to her, "Don't touch me. I have not yet ascended to my Father. Go to my brothers and say to them, 'I am ascending to my Father and your Father, to my God and your God.'"

She went back to the disciples. "I have seen the Lord!" she announced. Then she reported what He had said to her. But they didn't believe her.

Meanwhile, as the other women had been hurrying to tell the disciples, Jesus had met them on their way and detained them. He said to them, "Hail!" They came up to Him and embraced His feet and worshipped Him. He said to them, "Don't be afraid. Go tell my brothers that they are to set out for Galilee. They will see me there."

The women brought the news to the Apostles and all the others, arriving on the heels of Mary Magdalen, but in all the confusion the whole story seemed madness to them, and they didn't believe them either.

Later in the day Jesus appeared to two of the disciples on their way to a village named Emmaeus, about seven miles from Jerusalem. At first they didn't know Him. But when He broke bread with them, "their eyes were opened." Then He vanished.

They got up immediately and returned to Jerusalem, where they found the eleven gathered together and the others with them. They were greeted with the words, "The Lord has risen indeed, and has appeared to Simon!" For Jesus had indeed appeared to Peter, the Prince of the Apostles, earlier that day, after he had left the tomb. But then they themselves began to relate what had happened to them on their journey, and how they had recognized Him in the breaking of the bread.

But even then there were some among the disciples who did not believe.

So when it was late that same day, though the doors where the disciples gathered had been closed for fear of the Jews, Jesus suddenly stood among them and said to them, "Peace to you! It is I, do not be afraid." When He had said this, He showed them His hands and His side.

He scolded them for their lack of faith and hardness of heart, in that they had not believed those who had seen him after He had risen.

In their panic, they thought they were seeing a ghost. He said to them, "Why are you so upset, and why do you have doubts in your hearts? See my hands and feet, that it is I myself. Feel me, and see. A ghost does not have flesh and bones as you see I have." But as they still disbelieved and marvelled for joy, He said, "Have you anything here to eat?" They offered Him a piece of broiled fish and a honeycomb. When He had eaten in their presence, He took what was left and gave it to them.

They were filled with joy at the sight of Him. He said to them, "These are the words I spoke to you while I was still with you, that everything had to be fulfilled which was written in the Law of Moses and the Prophets and the Psalms about me." Then He opened their minds, for them to understand the Scriptures.

He said to them again, "Peace to you! As the Father has sent me, I also send you." When He had said this, He breathed on them and said to them, "Receive the Holy Spirit. Whose sins you shall forgive, they are forgiven them. Whose sins you shall retain, they are retained."

Now Thomas, one of the Twelve, called the Twin, was not with them when Jesus came. So the other disciples later said to him, "We have seen the Lord!" But he answered, "Unless I see in His hands the print of the nails, and put my finger into the place of the nails, and put my hand into His side, I will not believe."

Then eight days later, the following Sunday, the disciples were again inside, and this time Thomas was with them. Jesus came, with the doors closed, and stood among them, and said, "Peace to you!" Then He said to Thomas, "Bring here your finger, and see my hands; and bring here your hand, and put it into my side. And be not unbelieving, but believing." Thomas answered, "My Lord and my God!" Jesus said to him, "Because you have seen me, you have believed. Blessed are they who have not seen, and yet have believed."

Later Jesus appeared again at the Sea of Tiberias in Galilee. Here's how He appeared. Simon Peter and Thomas and Nathanael and the sons of Zebedee and two others of His disciples were together. Simon Peter said to them, "I'm going fishing." They said to him, "We'll go with you." They all went out and got into the boat. That night they caught nothing. But when day was breaking, Jesus stood on the beach. Yet the disciples didn't know it was Jesus.

He said to them, "Children, have you caught any fish?" They answered Him, "No." He said to them, "Throw the net to the right of the boat and you'll find them." So they did, and now they were unable to haul it up for the great number of fish. John said to Peter, "It's the Lord!" Simon Peter, on hearing that it was the Lord, pulled his tunic over him, for he was stripped, and threw himself into the sea. The other disciples came with the boat - for they weren't far from land, only about a hundred yards - dragging the net full of fish.

When they had landed, they saw a fire ready and a fish laid on it and bread. Jesus said to them, "Bring here some of the fish you caught just now." Simon Peter went aboard and hauled the net onto the land, full of large fish, one hundred and fifty-three in number. And though there were so many, the net was still not torn.

Jesus said to them, "Come and breakfast." None of them dared ask Him, "Who are you?" knowing that it was the Lord. Jesus took the bread and gave it to them, and likewise the fish.

This was now the third time that He had appeared to the disciples after rising from the dead.

When they had had breakfast, Jesus said to Simon Peter, "Simon, son of John, do you love me more than these do?" He said to Him, "Yes, Lord, You know that I love You." He said to him, "Feed my lambs." Then He said to him a second time, "Simon, son of John, do you love me?" He said to Him, "Yes, Lord, You know that I love You." He said to him, "Feed my lambs." A third time He said to him, "Simon, son of John, do you love me?" Peter was upset that

He had said to him a third time, "Do you love me?" and he said to Him, "Lord, You know everything! You know that I love You!" He said to him, "Feed my sheep."

Jesus went on, "I tell you the truth, when you were young you put a belt on and walked where you would. But when you are old, you will stretch out your hands, and another will tie you fast and lead you where you would rather not go." He said this to indicate by what kind of death he would glorify God. Then He said to him, "Follow me."

Peter turned around and saw John following them. He said to Jesus, "Lord, what about him?" Jesus said to him, "If I want him to remain until I come, what is it to you? You follow me."

The word went out among the disciples because of this that John was not going to die. But that's not what Jesus had said.

After this, the eleven were all together at the mountain in Galilee where Jesus had directed them to go. He appeared to them there, and they worshipped Him. He came up to them and spoke to them in these words: "All power in Heaven and on earth has been given to me. Go into the whole world, and preach the good news to everyone. Make disciples of all nations, and baptize them in the name of the Father and of the Son and of the Holy Spirit. Teach them to observe all that I have commanded you. Whoever believes and is baptized will be saved, but whoever does not believe will be condemned. Signs like these will accompany those who believe: in my name they will cast out devils; they will speak new languages; they will be able to handle serpents; and if they drink any deadly thing, it won't hurt them; they will lay hands on the sick, and they will get well. And behold, I am with you all through the days that are coming, even to the end of the world."

Later, Jesus appeared to five hundred of the disciples at once. He also appeared to James.

Then, finally, after forty days had passed, He appeared to them in Jerusalem again and said to them, "Thus it is written, that the Christ should suffer, and should rise again from the dead on the third day, and that repentance and forgiveness of sins should be preached in His name to all the nations, beginning from Jerusalem. You yourselves are witnesses of these things. I am sending down on you the promise of my Father. But wait here in the city until you are clothed with power from On High. For you will receive power when the Holy Spirit comes upon you, and you will be witnesses for me in Jerusalem and in all Judea and Samaria and even to the ends of the earth."

Then He led them out toward Bethany and lifted up His hands and blessed them. As He was blessing them, He parted from them and was carried up into Heaven, and sits at the right hand of God.

They worshipped Him. Then they returned to Jerusalem with great joy.

Ten days later the Holy Spirit would come to the assembled community of 120 or so believers. He would fill them with fortitude and fire, and they would begin to go out and preach to the whole world.

Christianity was born.

+

In meditating on the Resurrection Victory of Our Lord Jesus Christ, perhaps the first thing we should note is that it was by His miracles that He proved that He was Divine, and principally by this miracle or "sign" of His glorious Resurrection from death.

The resurrection of Jesus from death is a true miracle. It is a "sign" that has the intrinsic power to demonstrate to every sincere and honest mind that He truly is what He claimed to be, the Divine Son of the Divine Father.

But having said this we must go on to say that the Resurrection is far more. It is a Mystery, a Mystery of grace and life, a Mystery of faith. Despite all its intrinsic power to convince human reason, the grace of the Holy Spirit must be present to the human mind and heart for a person to be able to make the act of faith in the Divinity of Christ.

But for us who have the immense good fortune to believe in Jesus, the Resurrection is a "Liturgical" Mystery of profound joy and peace and strength.

We say to one another on Easter Sunday morning, "Christ is risen!" And it is a prayer of happiness, a thrilling act of worship.

By His Resurrection Christ not only "proved His Divinity" for the theology textbooks to record until the end of time. He did this, surely. But what He really did was to win. He won the victory! For all of us, for all ages. He won the victory over sin, death and every other evil.

Christ's Resurrection is the Victory of Life. It is the Victory of Peace for every human heart that comes to know and believe in Him as the Savior of all.

Christ is risen! The world has been created anew! Our despairing world is now a world rejoicing in the fullness of hope.

We are still free. We are still capable of sinning, even seriously - but we have Jesus! In the Church, in the Eucharist, in all the sacraments. We have the power of His Holy Spirit at our disposal, "for the forgiveness of sins" and the making of saints. And we have Mary, the Mother of God, to confirm us in fidelity.

There is no excuse now for spiritual failure. God has done for us everything that needed to be done. He has repaired sin superabundantly. *Copiosa apud Eum redemptio*. He has redeemed us all "copiously." We are lacking in no grace at all that we need either for salvation or sanctity. We have only to go to Jesus Christ, in His Spirit, in His Church, in prayer.

He is ever and totally available - in the Eucharist, in the priest, in our brothers and sisters of the Catholic Community, in quiet, confident prayer.

Christ is risen! Success is certain, for each and every one of us who truly desires it. He promises holiness and happiness, spiritual greatness, eternal victory to all who follow Him along the way of prayer, or the way of sincere faith, or the way of confidence and love or whatever path of humility and truth in which His Holy Spirit may lead us. He will enable us to make it a way of fidelity and perseverance in grace and justice and growth to the very end.

Jesus promises that He will be with us to the very end. We have heard His voice, "I am with you all days...!" All His infinite Divine Power is at our disposal. We have only to go to Him and cling to Him as little children in absolute dependence and confidence.

He Himself will be our Humility and our Fortitude.

He has fought for us and won. That victory will never be reversed. It is eternal.

And it is complete. He will make us not only holy, but also truly and perfectly whole, beginning within, from the deepest depths of our soul, from the center outward to the fullest extensions of our being. He is the radiantly Risen One, and He can give us a human smile bright with His own Divine Blessedness.

He is our King. He is the Prince of Life. He is the Winner. He is True God and True Man. And He loves us.

We must tell ourselves these things many times. For faith, and growth in faith, do not come naturally. We must meditate very much on the goodness and power of God, in order that we may believe ever more and more in the greatness and reality of His love for us, and in order that He may lead us on from there to the gift of prayer.

Christ is risen! The whole universe has been renewed. The power of the Risen Jesus reaches to the farthest corners of the cosmos. He is Lord of All.

Itaque epulemur. Let us rejoice and be glad. "Rejoice in the Lord always! Again I say, Rejoice!" Rejoice in the grace and gift of the Resurrection, the grace and gift of Life.

We know now that in every crucifixion of our soul or body, we have only to be very businesslike and wait. After every crucifixion a resurrection will follow. After every painful death there will follow a new and more wonderfully joyful life. After every suffering, after every agony, after every anguish, there will follow a deeper and truer and purer peace.

The "dark night" itself we have only patiently to "wait

out," spending it with Mary, our Blessed and Beautiful Virgin Mother, and there will come the bright and happy Dawn.

Christ is risen! The Sun of Justice shines once again, and now forever. Even into this dark world, in which we live by the obscure light of faith, His radiant beams penetrate sufficiently to make us strong and confident.

"God is with us." Ever since His Incarnation in the womb of Mary by the power of His Holy Spirit, He has been with us. Even in death the Divinity did not abandon our world, but remained with the Body of Jesus in the tomb, while His Human Soul was visiting the Limbo of the Fathers to deliver the just who awaited Him.

And now that He is risen and has sent us His Holy Spirit, He is more with us than ever, in grace, in our victorious faith, in the Blessed Sacrament. He is with us in our sense of His Presence. He is with us in His promises, in the power He gives us continually to "keep on keepin' on" toward the City of Eternal Joy, the Beautiful Kingdom of Heaven.

So we walk on. We are following Him who has gone before us. It is a way of crucifixion and of resurrection. We keep moving forward in the certainty of faith, hope and love.

Jesus Himself is the Way. Mary is our Guide along the Way. Joseph is our Protector.

We can see it ahead, the All Beautiful City, the Beloved City, the Blessed Land of Promise.

Heaven! Our hearts are already there! The anchor of hope is fixed for us there, beyond the veil that hides the Mysterious Reality from our eyes.

We see the unseen by faith in Jesus Christ, crucified and risen.

We see what the world is simply incapable of seeing. We see because we believe.

Without faith in Jesus Christ it is impossible to see all that there is to be seen. And there is a lot to be seen, even though we see in darkness and obscurity, in unsatisfying faith.

Essentially, what we see is God, in Jesus Christ. We see the goodness, wisdom and power of the Father in "this Jesus" who became One of us, who triumphed over sin and death, and now awaits us in the Kingdom of Heaven.

By faith we see Him ahead of us, encouraging us to keep advancing, onward, ever onward, toward the City where He rules by Absolute Love.

He is our Hope. He is the Kingdom we seek.

Because we can see by faith, our hope is great and profound. It is "joyful hope." It is love impatiently running toward our Divine Future.

"Christ has died. Christ is risen. Christ will come again."

The Church invites us in her Liturgy to "hasten" it by prayer. Truly it is all we live for. It is "the Still-to-come." It is Jesus.

Forgetting all that lies behind, as St. Paul said, leaving the past to God's mercy, as St. Augustine said, we press forward toward the Goal, trying with all our might to assist God's unfolding Providence.

The Day of the Lord will come in His good time. Yet we desire to be ready. For if He finds us watching, it will be an utterly blessed Day.

We know that sin is the only death, and we look forward to Life, as we pray the prayer of expectation, "Come, Lord Jesus!"

Maran atha. "The Lord is coming." It is truer than we realize. It is always later than we think.

We are on our way, even now, to meet Him. Our joy is real because He is most real.

He has tried us, and taught us, and we have learned to believe. We have come to realize that in the most important sense nothing more is necessary. "Only believe!"

Our living faith is our hope and our love. Our dependence on Jesus Christ is absolute. In prayer we wait, for His coming.

Conclusion

This Is the Victory

The story of Jesus has been told many times, more or less well. In telling it once again, in the sense of meditating on it, this book has tried to say that the holiness of God is, or is found in, the wholeness of Jesus. We have remarked it all throughout the ministry of His public life. "Go in peace. Your faith has made you whole." It is always to living faith that Christ's gift of wholeness is given.

Yes, "This is the victory that overcomes the world, our faith." Jesus is our Victorious Savior. "In the world you will have distress. But Confidence! I have overcome the world." Our faith in Him makes us too victorious, sharers in His own victory.

It makes us whole. This is the meaning of victory. "This is the victory" over the world, the flesh and the devil, over "sex, drugs and alcohol," over everything - "our faith."

And how does it make us victorious? Through suffering. We have seen that the sequel to Christ's public ministry, what we may truly call His "ministry of wholeness," was His crucifixion and death. We entitled this third section of the book, "Integrity." For Jesus was true even to death.

Holiness, wholeness, integrity - this is for us the

ethic of living faith, as it was for Jesus the story of His whole life in this world.

He is indeed The Whole Man. He is holy with the holiness of Divinity. He is whole with the wholeness of the most perfect of humans. And in His obedience and fidelity to the will of the Father He is for us all the Model of absolute moral, intellectual and spiritual integrity, even to death.

Wholeness - we find it only in Christ. We find it only in faith in Him, in absolute Eucharistic dependence on Him, our Lord and our God. We find it only in religion, only in worship, only in prayer.

We find it only in the holiness of humility and in the integrity of suffering. We find the wholeness of faith in the Risen Jesus only in the humiliation and purification of self-emptying and pain. We advance to Resurrection and Life only through crucifixion and death.

But the way of living faith is truly a way of victory, and we find the wholeness of Jesus even in this world, after each crucifixion that we go through, in the resurrection that always follows.

It is not the perfect wholeness of Heaven. It is not even the perfect gift of integrity that Adam had in the beginning before the fall. Yet in a sense it is something even greater than Adam's gift. The Church teaches in her Liturgy that the grace of Christ somehow, mysteriously, gives us "a greater dignity than we had in the beginning." It is in fact precisely the honor and privilege of suffering with Jesus and for love of Him that gives us this "greater dignity" and the integrity or wholeness that is so truly wonderful in God's saints.

It is living faith in Jesus, and love for Him, that enables the saints of the New Covenant to rise to spiritual heights that truly surpass, in the most important sense, the situation of Adam in the state of original justice.

Truly do we sing, "O Happy Fault! Which merited such and so great a Redeemer!" Truly can St. Paul say that "where sin abounded, grace abounded more," not merely more than the original sin, but in some very mysterious way - explainable only in the order of love, the grace of love - even more than the original grace.

This is the order of dignity, as the Paschaltide prayer quoted above gives us the clue. Perhaps only in our own day is the Church fully realizing and proclaiming to all nations the profound dignity of each and every individual human person. But man's greatest dignity, his full and perfect holiness and wholeness, is achieved only through humiliation and suffering after the pattern of Jesus, the Savior.

St. Paul said it well: "Our warring is not against flesh and blood, but against principalities and powers, the evil spirits in the heavens, the rulers of this dark world." Our struggle is that of Jesus - to be true. Our struggle is for complete and perfect integrity.

Christ could not deny His own Divinity. "Before Abraham came to be, I AM."

We cannot deny Him, who is the Truth.

Being true to Himself brought Him to crucifixion and death.

Being true to Him will bring us the same.

But even in this world, because He won the first big Victory, there will be for us little victories all along the way. It seems that we may say that our victories will become greater and greater all along the way - if we persevere in prayer - even if the crucifixions also become more terrible and more purifying, till we too achieve by God's grace the final and eternal victory over all death.

It is our victories over sin that assure us of this final victory over death. If we are victorious over sin, what the world calls death, the death of the body, will mean for us only the blessed transition to perfect, unending Life.

Jesus promises us the victory: "Ask and you shall receive, seek and you shall find...." And so we pursue our life of prayer in hope and in love for Him. But then one day the wonderful Holy Spirit, by His gift of understanding, enables us to see that we already have the victory in "our faith." And we realize that to reach eternal joy we need only continue quietly along the very path we have been following. We realize now that it really is the way of victory.

And so we go on. "Knock and the door will be opened to you." Our prayer has become a continual "knocking," that the Door of God's Heavenly Paradise may be soon opened to us.

The prayer of faith has brought us many graces. It brought us the grace to surrender to God. It brought us the graces of simple union and of transformation into Jesus. And then finally it became for us the grace of victory.

Do we dare call this the grace of perfect love?

It is the grace of victory. Let us be content to continue living by faith. For we know that we love, and we know that perfection itself is nothing more than love.

Jesus, the Whole Man, has brought us the gift of wholeness. Let us be simple little children and ask no more questions. It is really all love.

Our faith itself is all shot through with love. Yet it is a love that not merely goes on "marrying and giving in marriage" until the end, but one that likewise believes in Jesus Christ, in God His Father and in Their wonderful Holy Spirit - to the end, so that as our ultimate conclusion we may truly say that when Jesus comes again He will indeed find "faith on the earth."

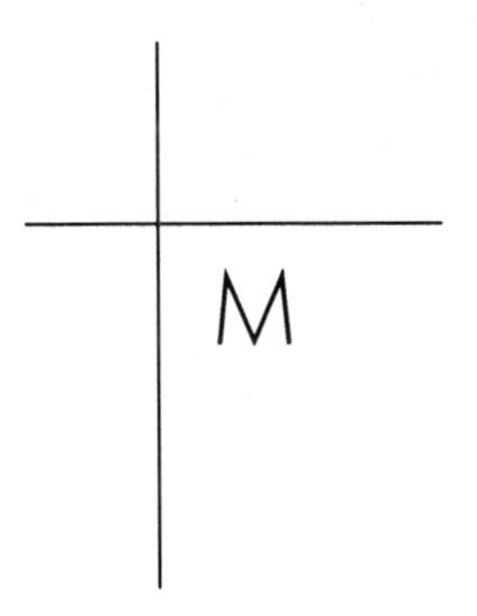